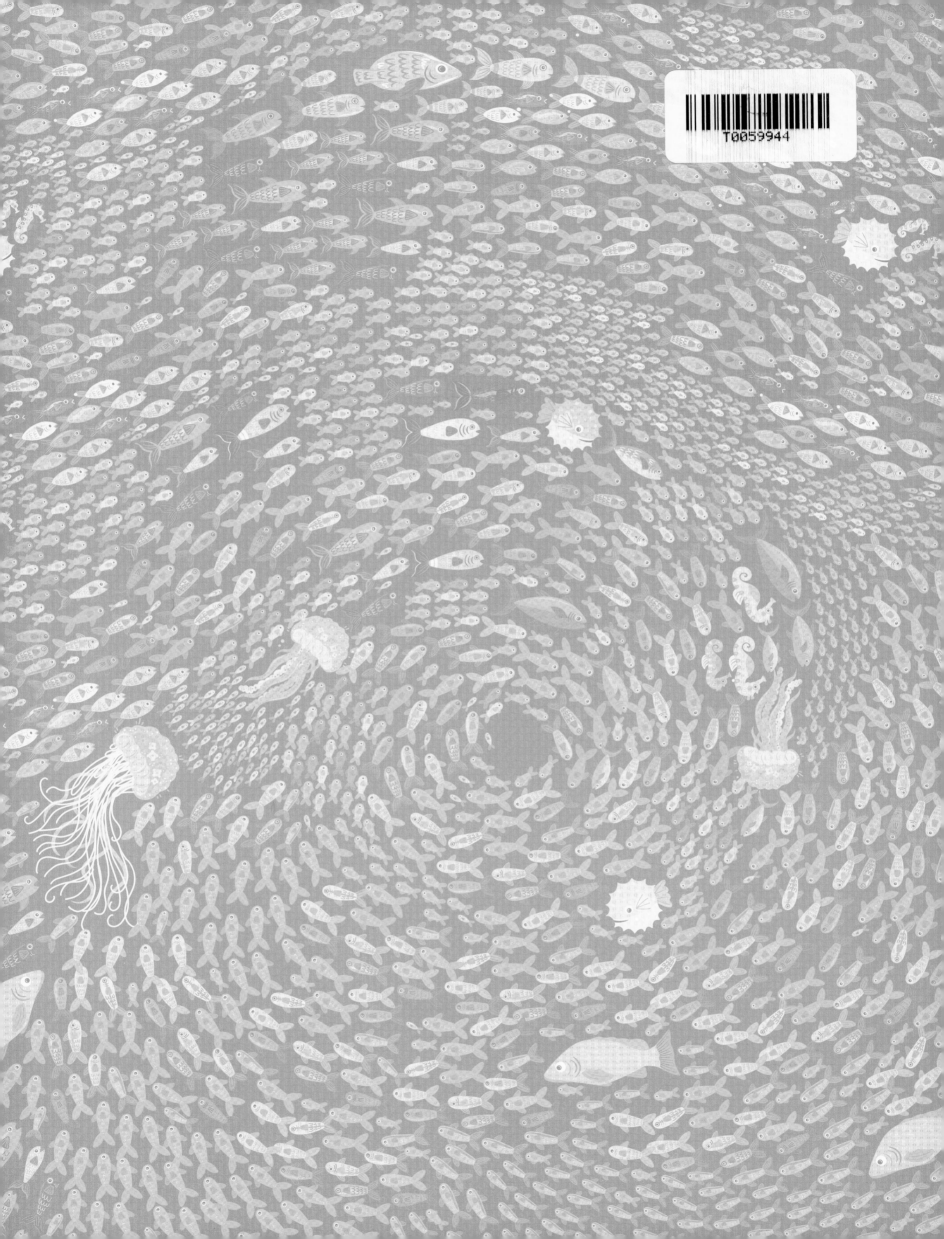

CINDY FORDE

ILLUSTRATED BY BETHANY LORD

# BRIGHT NEW WORLD

W

WELBECK
EDITIONS

For
Alaïs, Chloé, Julian, Leo, Lilah, Lilly, Mia and Sophie
And for Saxon, Tasman and Everest.
C.F.

Dedicated to all the children out there inspired to make change!
B.L.

ABOUT PLANETARI
Planetari is an education platform dedicated to equipping children to understand
how Earth works and how they can be part of creating a brighter world.
**www.planetari.world**

Published in 2022 by Welbeck Editions

An imprint of Welbeck Children's Limited,
part of Welbeck Publishing Group.
20 Mortimer Street, London, W1T 3JW

ISBN 978 1 80338 047 6

Printed in Dongguan, China

10 9 8 7 6 5 4 3 2 1

FSC
www.fsc.org
MIX
Paper | Supporting
responsible forestry
FSC® C144853

# FOREWORD

I've been campaigning on environmental issues for more than 50 years. But my world changed on August 20, 2018 when a 16-year-old schoolgirl in Stockholm decided to go on strike—to remind Swedish politicians that they simply weren't doing enough to address the Climate Emergency. By the end of 2019, around seven million young people had joined Greta Thunberg, in one way or another, in urging politicians the world over to get their act together. Then we were held up by Covid, but this is still one of the most inspirational movements I've ever seen. It made me more hopeful than anything else over the last few years. Young people standing up, so courageously, to remind their parents' and grandparents' generation that they've made a real mess of things so far—in terms of protecting this beautiful and fragile planet of ours.

I know just how passionately many young people feel about the environment—and I hate the fact that so much of what they hear about it is all the bad stuff: the disasters, the extinction of species, the pollution, and climate change apparently just getting worse and worse. It really shouldn't be like that.

Which is why I really love *Bright New World*. It doesn't ignore any of the problems—that wouldn't help anyone. But it then invites us in to celebrate all the amazing things that are happening, all the brilliant campaigns (and young campaigners!), the stories of hope from around the world, and the special places that are protected, restored and loved.

And what's the most amazing thing of all? Every time we put Nature first (rather than prioritising yet more development and growth), we get so many other benefits: we get cleaner air and cleaner water, less waste, livelihoods and communities better protected, and more of those wretched greenhouse gases stored in soils, trees, and vegetation, rather than ending up in the atmosphere.

We now know just how important this is. We know we have to put Nature back at the heart of our lives—in our towns and cities as much as in rural areas or wild places. And we know that all this puts joy in our hearts and a smile on our faces. And we need a lot more joy and many more smiles in such a troubled and destructive world.


Jonathan Porritt, author and campaigner

# CONTENTS

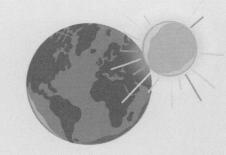

# INTRODUCTION
## A WORLD THAT WORKS FOR EVERYONE

Beautiful, isn't it? Our tiny planet, in our enormous solar system, contains the only known life in the whole universe.

Each of our parts in the planet's life is important. Yours is perhaps the most important of all.

Humans face serious problems like climate change, species extinction, global pandemics, diminishing rainforests, polluted oceans, poverty, and inequality in many forms. Every form of life here is threatened, including ours, because Earth is finding it harder to do her job of looking after us all.

But because we now understand much more about how our planet works, we know how we can create a brighter world where all life can flourish.

In this book, we're going to visit that brighter world.

We'll explore the wonderful future we can have if we use our heads, and hearts, and dare to think differently. We know Earth is our life support system. So what if we turned the things that have caused the problems into the solutions? Energy, food, farms, factories, cities, buildings, trains, planes, cars. How we care for our rainforests, our oceans, each other, other creatures. How we take vacations, what we learn in school, what we choose to buy—it's all important.

Most of the solutions we need to do this already exist.

EARTH

Many are already at work, and others are on the drawing board. We'll look back from a world where our major problems are solved, then explore the steps that will get us there.

By working together with a shared purpose, just imagine what we can do! It's already happening. In 2015, almost every country agreed to the United Nations' Sustainable Development Goals, 17 goals that point us to a brighter world by 2030. This book is a roadmap to help us on our way.

It's a map you will be part of making.

You'll get to join in and help imagine how things can be done, and to invent solutions of your own. Remember we are together on this journey. And just imagine how Earth will be even more beautiful when our star shines out into the universe in the years to come.

# THE FUTURE IS BRIGHT
## THIS IS THE WORLD WE COULD MAKE!

Hi, and welcome to the future! Read on, and find out what life could be like in the years to come...

"After that big scare when we only had about 10 years to stop our planet's temperature rising by more than 2.7 degrees, we all worked together, really fast. We agreed that we'd judge success on how healthy our planet is and how well cared for its citizens are—human and otherwise. We're doing pretty well, just look!"

"People realized that only counting how much money things made had caused most of the problems. It made some of us very rich, but many very poor. Though we could buy things cheaply, it almost cost the Earth."

"Now we design everything to cause no harm, or better still, help Earth regenerate. We power everything by the sun, wind, or waves. Our farms are vertical and our cities grow health and happiness. "Living" buildings power themselves, produce zero emissions, and clean the air."

"Sea levels have stopped rising, but we've kept our floating cities and towns. They help make sure everyone has a home and bring us closer to our heroes—the oceans! Now rainforests and oceans are internationally protected treasures. We look after the web of life that looks after us."

"Thinking differently has made this bright future possible. To tell the truth, we'd known for a long time what needed to be done and most solutions were already there. So we just got busy and did it!"

# A CONNECTED WORLD

All life on Earth is interconnected. It's a living planet. Like any living thing, what happens in one part of the system affects the other.

Over billions of years, life on Earth has transformed and the climate has changed naturally. But in recent years, human activity has affected Earth's ability to stay in balance and to remain a safe place for humans and all other forms of life.

## EARTH'S PROBLEMS

### So what's causing these problems?

The sun is the source of warmth for Earth. Ice and clouds reflect some of this heat away as light. The rest is captured by our oceans and land and warms these surfaces. Some heat escapes to space, but most is absorbed by greenhouse gases in our atmosphere.

They are called greenhouse gases because they trap heat and keep Earth warm. We need these gases, like carbon dioxide ($CO_2$), methane, and water vapor, to keep our planet at just the right temperature.

Over millions of years, the amount of $CO_2$ in the atmosphere has changed. But, since the industrial revolution in the late 18th century, when we started to use fossil fuels, such as oil, coal, and natural gas, to power our factories, homes, and transport, we've put about 2,000 gigatons* of $CO_2$ into the atmosphere. So more and more heat is getting trapped in Earth's atmosphere.

* 1 gigaton = the weight of 12.2 billion people (twice the world's population!)

There are now almost 8 billion people on Earth, up from just over 1 billion 100 years ago. We are clearing more land to build more cities. To have space to raise all the animals we eat, we are chopping down forests. Forests are carbon sinks which means they absorb $CO_2$. Without them, even more heat gets trapped. And dead trees release the carbon they once stored. More heat!

About half of the habitable land on Earth has been cleared for agriculture, much of this for raising cows. When cows burp, they let out methane which is a greenhouse gas. More heat!

The oceans absorb huge amounts of heat. They are the planet's best carbon sinks. Because the planet is warming, they are absorbing more heat than ever before. This makes them too acidic which damages the coral reefs which help store carbon and keep the oceans healthy. And because of overfishing, many sea creatures that help absorb and store carbon are gone, so even more carbon escapes to heat Earth.

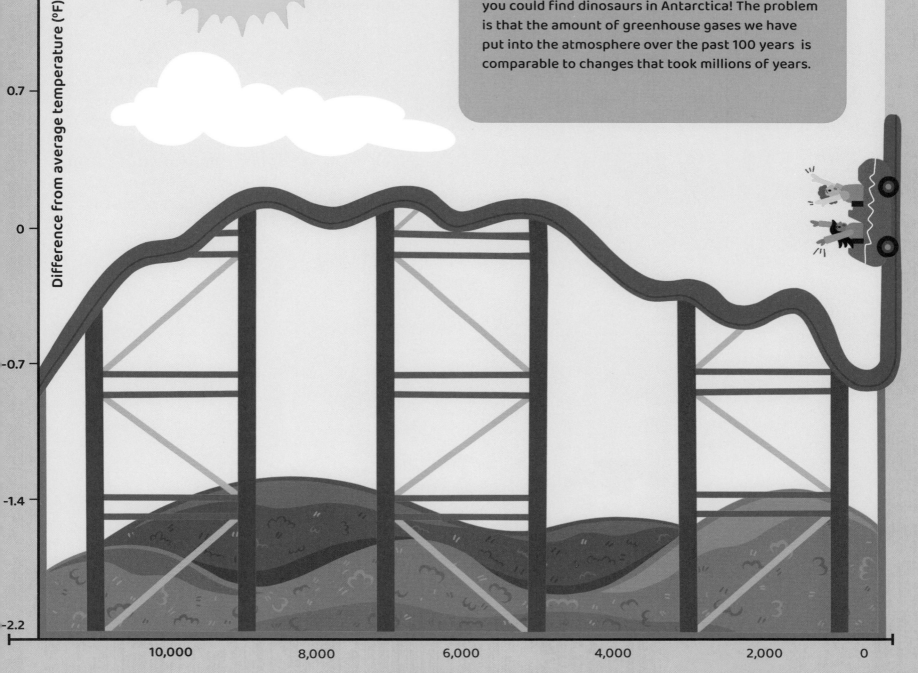

# ROLLER COASTER DANGER

As the planet heats, ice caps and polar regions melt. This means they can't reflect heat away from Earth as light and also causes sea levels to rise.

If we keep emitting greenhouse gases and destroying our natural carbon sinks, our world will keep getting warmer. Earth has experienced ice ages and has also seen extremely warm periods, where you could find dinosaurs in Antarctica! The problem is that the amount of greenhouse gases we have put into the atmosphere over the past 100 years is comparable to changes that took millions of years.

*If it was a roller coaster, the temperature rise would look like this:*

**Difference from average temperature (°F)**

1.4
0.7
0
-0.7
-1.4
-2.2

10,000   8,000   6,000   4,000   2,000   0

**Years before present**

# LIFE CYCLES

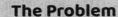

Knowing how our planet works helps us learn to live in balance with it. Whatever we may want to be—farmers, physicists, filmmakers—we need to do it in a way that causes no more harm. Or better still, in a way that helps Earth regenerate!

Let's look at two vital cycles so we understand how to work with them:

## THE CARBON CYCLE

Carbon is an element formed from exploding stars. It's in every living thing, including you. Earth constantly takes in, stores, and releases carbon. Like breathing! It's the most important building block for all life on this planet. For a healthy Earth, we need the right amount of carbon in the atmosphere.

### The Problem

Since fossil fuels have increasingly powered our world, carbon that Earth took millions of years to store has been released in a few hundred. This makes Earth too hot. The carbon cycle is out of balance.

Stop putting more $CO_2$ into the atmosphere, by changing how we produce energy.

### The Solutions

Get $CO_2$ out of the atmosphere, by looking after our carbon sinks. Carbon sinks absorb carbon from the atmosphere and reduce the amount of $CO_2$ in the air. The main natural carbon sinks are oceans, forests, plants and soil, and bogs.

1. Plants use sunlight to turn $CO_2$ in the atmosphere into glucose, a form of sugar. This is called photosynthesis. Glucose is used as energy to power the whole food chain.

6. More energy comes from the sun to feed new plants and animals.

3. Bigger animals eat the smaller ones.

2. Animals eat the plants.

4. When animals and plants die, they sink into the earth, or sea.

5. Over millions of years, carbon trapped inside the fossilized remains of these animals and plants turns into coal, oil, or natural gas.

**Evaporation**
Rivers, lakes, and oceans absorb heat from the sun. As the water gets hotter, some of it turns into a gas called vapor.

**Condensation**
As water vapor rises into the sky, it cools off and turns back into droplets which form together as clouds.

**Precipitation**
When a lot of water has condensed into clouds, they get too heavy to hold the water. It falls back down to earth as rain, sleet, hail, or snow.

**Transpiration**
Plants and trees lose water through their leaves.

**Collection**
Water is collected in rivers, lakes, oceans, and plants, and the cycle continues.

# THE WATER CYCLE

What have you got in common with a saber-tooth tiger, Queen Cleopatra, and Chief Sitting Bull? You drink the same water. Earth has recycled water for over 4 billion years.

## The Problem

As more $CO_2$ gets into the atmosphere, Earth gets warmer so:

- More water evaporates into the air. Warmer air can hold more water vapour, which can lead to severe rainstorms, causing major problems like flooding.

- In some places, air gets drier, which means trees and plants and even the soil dries out. So when it does rain, much of the water runs off the hard ground into rivers and streams, and the soil remains dry, increasing risks of drought and fires.

- Ice at the North and South Poles is melting. This puts more water vapor into the atmosphere, so things get even hotter. It also puts more water into the sea which causes sea levels to rise, increasing the risk of severe flooding.

**The Solutions**

**Use and waste less water.**

**Cut greenhouse gas emissions.**

# CLIMATE CHANGE

**What happens when the climate changes—even by a little bit?**

This is the saddest part of this book. But it can make us determined to do things differently, which is what this book is about.

The world's average temperature is now about 1.8 degrees Fahrenheit higher than it was before the industrial revolution, 200 years ago. It sounds small, but it makes a big difference. It's already changed our planet.

All the different effects and changes are connected to each other. To solve climate change, we need to work with our living Earth to restore a balance across the whole system. It's not just about reducing carbon emissions—we need to restore and care for our people, forests, rivers and oceans, and the creatures who live there.  All these have a vital role to play in a healthy planet.

## EFFECTS OF CLIMATE CHANGE

STORMS, HURRICANES, AND CYCLONES

RISING SEA LEVELS

DROUGHT

FIRES

HEATWAVES

HEAVY RAINFALL

# CONSEQUENCES

### Disappearing places
As sea levels rise, low-lying areas (such as Pacific islands like the Maldives, and Fiji) are at risk of disappearing entirely. Cities like Jakarta in Indonesia, New York in the USA, Shanghai in China, and The Hague in the Netherlands could sink beneath sea water.

### Species extinction
Many of the world's threatened species live in areas severely affected by climate change. Climate change is happening too quickly for many species, both animal and plant, to adapt. Over 1 million species now face extinction.

### Freshwater pressure
Climate change unbalances the world's water systems causing flooding and droughts. In 2019, heavy rains left more than 45 million people in 14 countries in Africa struggling to find food. And floods in Bangladesh left over 200,000 people homeless.

### Devasted forests and communities
Drought, high temperatures, and high winds are a lethal combination for forests. In 2019-2020, Australian bushfires destroyed 12.5 million hectares of forest—that's the size of South Korea. Nearly three billion animals died or lost their home.

### Trouble at the poles
The North and South polar regions are crucial for regulating our planet. Antarctic ice is melting 6 times faster than 20 years ago. Sea ice could be gone from the Arctic within 15 years.

### Acidic oceans
The oceans are absorbing so much $CO_2$ that some waters are becoming too acidic. This can harm coral reefs and sea creatures. Over half the world's coral reefs have been lost or severely damaged.

### Loss of land, home, and country
After a disaster has destroyed their homes and livelihood, many people have to find another place, or even another country to live in. This is called displacement. An average of 22.5 million people have been displaced by climate or weather-related events every year since 2008.

### Health hazards
Air pollution due to burning of fossil fuels caused 8.7 million people's death globally in 2018, almost 4 times more than Covid-19.

# EFFECTS OF CLIMATE CHANGE

Scientists agree that if we stop global temperatures from rising by no more than another 0.9°F by the end of the century, we can prevent some of these effects at their worst.

If we don't, by the end of this century, the planet will have warmed by more than twice that amount with tragic consequences. Yet scientists also agree that we are due to pass the 2.7°F mark within the next 10 years! So we have to act fast.

The good news is, we already have almost all of the solutions, as we'll find out in the rest of this book.

# SUPER POWER
## THE FUTURE OF ENERGY

In your time, producing energy often means damaging the planet. But if you work together, you could have a future like this...

"We had a huge celebration all around the world last year and got a new international holiday, Sun Day. It's to commemorate that almost all power on Earth now comes directly from the sun."

"We've had solar tower power stations for ages, but the breakthrough came when we finally got artificial photosynthesis right. This means we can make liquid fuel directly from sunlight!"

"All our vehicles can now be transitioned to run completely on 'Sun'—that's what we call the new fuel. We don't need to mine rare minerals for electric vehicle batteries anymore. We're turning the mines into nature reserves."

"This 'Sun' is powerful enough to drive heavy vehicles like trucks, cargo ships, planes, and rockets, so we can phase out biofuels and hydrogen. Since we've had so much energy to go around, we have a much more peaceful world."

"We cleaned up the oceans, replanted the forests, and education and healthcare are free almost everywhere. Far less people get ill, and climate change has stabilized so there's more fresh water to go around. "

"The new photosynthesis technology is portable and cheap, so everybody agreed that 'Sun' should be free. It's funny, when you don't have to fight over something you get much better at sharing!"

# ENERGY FOR ALL

**Almost all energy on Earth comes from a single source: the sun.**

The sun has powered life on Earth since our planet was formed, billions of years ago. Yet the way humans have used this energy in the last 300 years has caused serious problems to almost every element of our world. Imagine if pirates took over a ship without understanding how to run the engine room. They'd soon hit the rocks!

Our mistakes have made us more humble about our place in this great system that is planet Earth, and we have learned from them. Instead of acting like pirates and wrecking the ship, we know now that we are crew along with many other amazing life forms. By learning how to use energy in harmony with nature, we can sail much more safely into the future.

## NONRENEWABLES

**Oil, coal, or natural gas are fossil fuels. They are burned by power stations to create steam which turns turbines and generates electricity.**

### Nuclear Power
Splitting uranium atoms in two releases heat. This heat produces steam, which turns turbines to generate electricity.  Nuclear power uses rare uranium which cannot be replaced. It also produces radioactive waste that is extremely harmful to living things and very hard to get rid of, so it's a very dangerous way of creating energy.

## POWERING OUR WORLD WISELY

### Troublemakers...
Nonrenewables take millions of years to form and to replace. They release greenhouse gases which cause the planet to heat.

### ...and Problem Solvers
Renewable energy can be collected from natural resources provided abundantly every day. They release fewer or no emissions.

# RENEWABLES

## Solar

Solar panels absorb energy from sunshine, creating electricity. This is fed into a "solar inverter" which converts it for direct use by houses or buildings, feeding any surplus into the energy grid to be shared.

## Wind

Turbines placed on hills, open plains, or out at sea can harness the power of wind. The wind turns specially designed blades that operate a generator which converts the energy from this movement, or kinetic energy, into electricity. It can be used locally or sent wherever needed via power lines.

## Hydro

Hydroelectric power stations are fueled by moving water. Generators placed in the path of fast flowing water extract this kinetic energy and turn it into electricity.

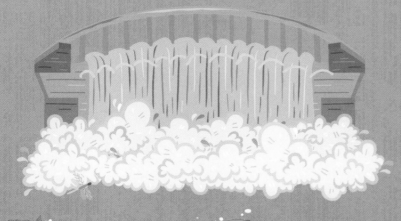

## Tidal

Tidal energy is wave power. Kinetic energy from the movement of the waves and daily swell of the tides is converted to electricity by a tidal generator.

## Geothermal

Deep within Earth's crust, hot water is stored. The deeper down, the hotter it is. At one to two miles' depth, its temperature is between 140 and 210°F. This hot water can be pumped up and the heat extracted using a heat exchanger and used to heat homes and buildings. The cooled water is then pumped back to eventually heat up again.

## Biomass

"Biomass" is any plant or animal material, which can generate electricity in different ways. Burning natural waste produces steam which can spin turbines, but this releases $CO_2$ and pollutes the air. Solid, liquid, or gas biofuels can be made by fermenting biomass. Though cleaner than petroleum, they still create some emissions.

## Green Hydrogen

Most hydrogen is produced from fossil fuels, usually natural gas which creates $CO_2$. Green hydrogen can be made by passing electric currents through water, leaving only oxygen as a by-product. It can be an important clean fuel. Used with fuel cells, it can power anything that uses electricity, including vehicles.

# A ZERO-CARBON FUTURE

The climate change initiative called Cambridge Zero is on a mission. They've joined up brilliant inventors, innovators, and researchers at the UK's Cambridge University and across the world, to work out how to create a planet with a zero-carbon future, leaving fossil fuels in the ground and in the past.

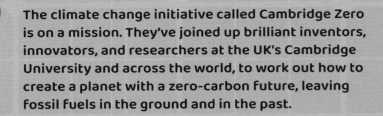

## TRANSFORMING ENERGY IS AT THE HEART OF THIS WORK

**HOW DO WE GO FROM THIS:**

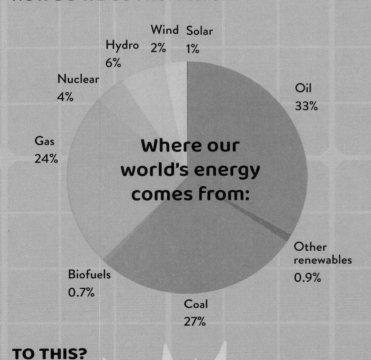

Where our world's energy comes from:

- Wind 2%
- Solar 1%
- Hydro 6%
- Nuclear 4%
- Gas 24%
- Biofuels 0.7%
- Oil 33%
- Other renewables 0.9%
- Coal 27%

**TO THIS?**

Solar powered
# 100%

Light from the sun contains enough energy to power the world 1,000 times over!

The sun is our only really abundant source of energy so it's vital that we figure out how to use it to power our world. The use of solar is growing, but we know there is a lot more we can do to use it more widely and efficiently.

Cambridge Zero is working on low-cost, next-generation solar cells which convert more of the sun's energy into electricity. They are also developing special types of batteries which can store this energy. So cars and machines can run on sunlight! It will be an energy revolution.

## POWERING UP

Here are just some of the ways that Cambridge Zero's researchers are trying to make power more planet-friendly.

### Printable power
The Stranks Lab is hard at work unpacking the power of perovskites. These are a kind of crystal found in nature, but that can easily be made in a lab. Manufactured as a very thin film, they use 20 times less resources than current silicon solar panels, and are much lighter. Imagine being able to "print" solar power onto the top of cars, boats, airplanes, or onto roofs, windows, rollable blinds, or even sails that double as solar panels!

### Taking a leaf from nature
Nature has a lot of the answers. Cambridge University's Department of Chemistry is figuring out how to use photosynthesis, the same process that plants use to turn sunlight into glucose, to turn sunlight into clean liquid fuel to power vehicles and industry. This "artificial leaf" contains a panel which reacts with sunlight, carbon dioxide, and water to make fuel.

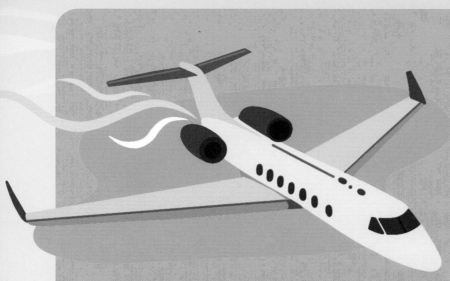

### The light fantastic
The Centre for Gallium Nitride is creating materials that do more with less. Gallium nitride is a manmade substance that can be used to make low energy light bulbs, which could make a huge difference to the amount of energy used around the world!

### Electrifying Aviation
At the Whittle Lab, engineers are developing light aircraft that can fully or partly run on electricity as well as the next generation of jet engines that can greatly reduce $CO_2$ emissions.

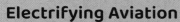

## ENERGY HEROES

Dr. Beth Tennyson and Dr. Stuart Mcpherson, post graduate researchers at Cambridge University's Stranks Lab, have set up the Primary School Energy Mapping Challenge. Budding young scientists across the UK measure sunlight and wind speed on their school playgrounds, to work out how much solar energy or wind energy could be collected if solar panels or a wind turbine were installed at their school. They then compare their data with that of the other participating schools, to figure out where in the UK is best to invest in solar or wind energy.

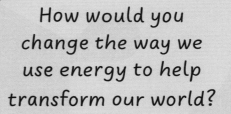

*How would you change the way we use energy to help transform our world?*

**What's your super power?**

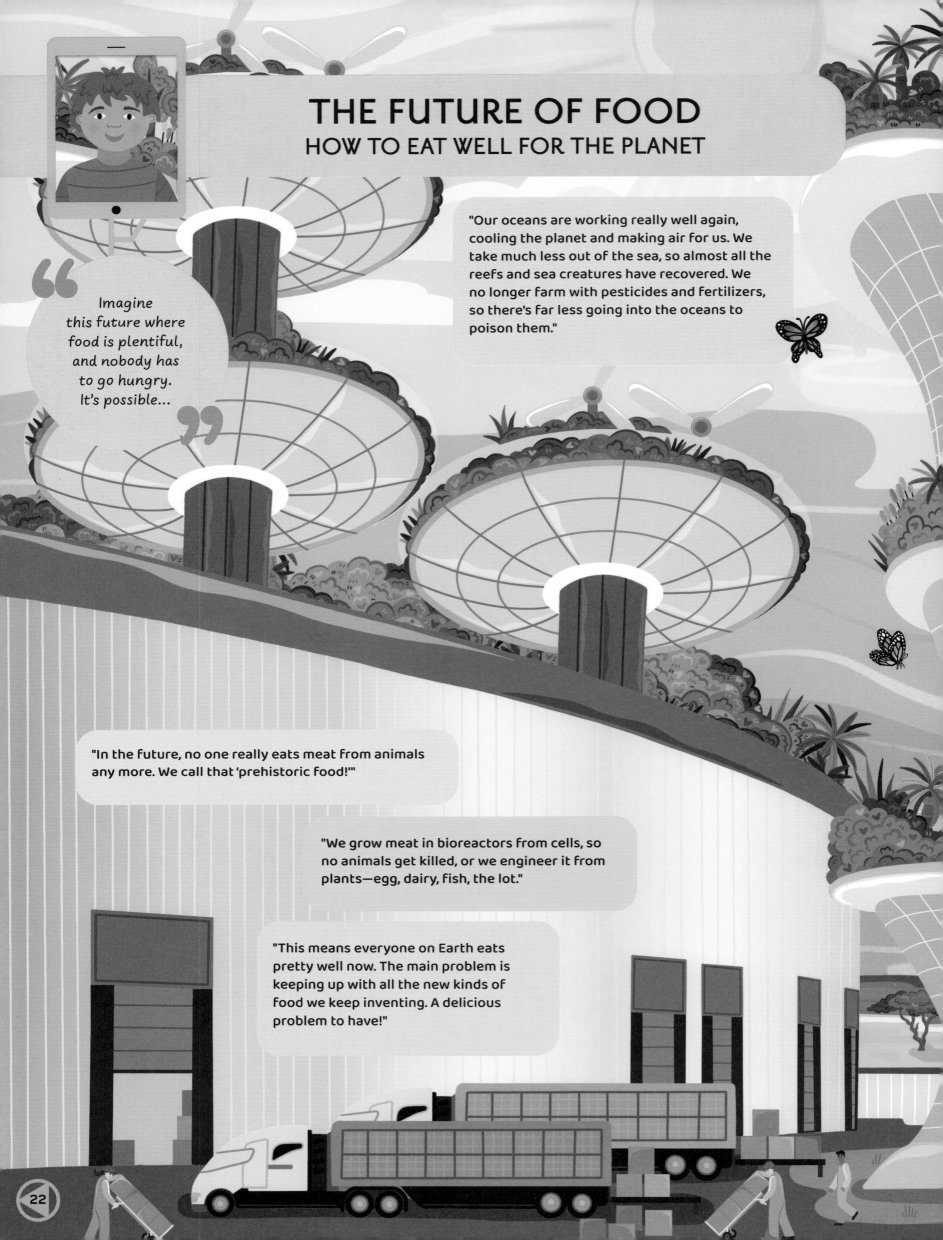

# THE FUTURE OF FOOD
## HOW TO EAT WELL FOR THE PLANET

"Imagine this future where food is plentiful, and nobody has to go hungry. It's possible…"

"Our oceans are working really well again, cooling the planet and making air for us. We take much less out of the sea, so almost all the reefs and sea creatures have recovered. We no longer farm with pesticides and fertilizers, so there's far less going into the oceans to poison them."

"In the future, no one really eats meat from animals any more. We call that 'prehistoric food!'"

"We grow meat in bioreactors from cells, so no animals get killed, or we engineer it from plants—egg, dairy, fish, the lot."

"This means everyone on Earth eats pretty well now. The main problem is keeping up with all the new kinds of food we keep inventing. A delicious problem to have!"

"Our farms are all regenerative or vertical, so we're either feeding the land as we grow food or growing it in stacked towers so there's more room for wild spaces that help keep our planet cool and healthy. And because we're not farming over half the habitable land on the planet, emissions are way down and climate change has stabilized."

"Our wild animals live pretty happily now they have much more space. Some came right back from the brink of extinction. We've even discovered incredible new species!"

# HAPPY EATING FOR EVERYONE

## WHAT'S THE SINGLE BIGGEST WAY TO HELP SOLVE OUR BIGGEST PROBLEMS?

## FOOD!

You need three key ingredients to make food: land, energy, and water. As there are so many more people in the world now, and some of us have gotten richer, we are eating more and more food. So we are using up more of these three things that are vital to all life on Earth.

So what's the recipe to make sure everyone in the world can eat well—in a way that also keeps Earth healthy?

### Wasting away!

Almost a third of the world's food gets wasted. 50 million chickens thown away, 100 million pints of milk down the drain every year, and that's just in the UK!

2 billion people can be fed by the 1.4 billion tons of food that is wasted by retailers and households around the world every year!

## TOO MUCH OF THE PIE

Half of the world's habitable land is used for agriculture. Earth is an interconnected, living system, so this has huge effects on almost every part of our planet. Understanding these effects helps us know what to do about them.

**26% of global greenhouse gas emissions come from making food**

**50% of global habitable land is used for agriculture**

**70% of global freshwater used is for agriculture**

**78% of global ocean and freshwater pollution is caused by use of fertilizers in agriculture**

**94% of the biomass (weight) of all mammals (excluding humans), is livestock**

# EATING EVERYTHING UP

Most mammals alive today are being raised to feed humans. With less and less other animals and plants, Earth's whole ecosystem becomes fragile and all life, including human life, is threatened.

- Each year we eat:
- 50 billion chickens
- 1.5 billion pigs
- Half a billion sheep
- Over 400 million goats
- About 150 million tons of seafood

## Hot stuff!
Raising the animals and harvesting the plants we eat, as well as the way we process, pack, and ship food to markets all over the world, is a major cause of climate change.

The emissions from producing meat are roughly equivalent to all the driving and flying of every car, truck, and plane in the world!

## What's the beef with beef?
This is the average amount of greenhouse gas (in pounds of $CO_2$) you need for 1.8 oz of protein:

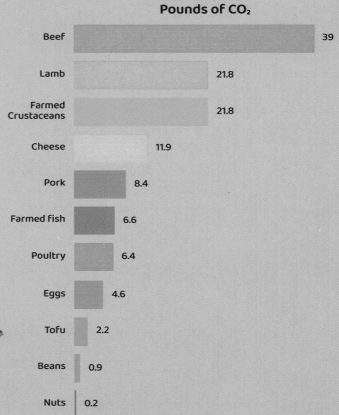

**Pounds of $CO_2$**

| | |
|---|---|
| Beef | 39 |
| Lamb | 21.8 |
| Farmed Crustaceans | 21.8 |
| Cheese | 11.9 |
| Pork | 8.4 |
| Farmed fish | 6.6 |
| Poultry | 6.4 |
| Eggs | 4.6 |
| Tofu | 2.2 |
| Beans | 0.9 |
| Nuts | 0.2 |

## Why do so many emissions come from beef and lamb?

- Growing crops to feed these animals takes a lot of land and energy.
- When cows digest food, they burp out methane, a greenhouse gas.

# THE MEAT MACHINE

## What has meat got to do with deforestation, rainforest fires, and viruses?

- Industrial meat is the single biggest cause of deforestation.
- Millions of acres of rainforest have been cleared to raise beef, or to grow crops to feed to animals.

- Farmers deliberately burn the forests to clear the land.
- Trees that could absorb the $CO_2$ are burned instead, releasing more carbon.
- Destroying forests brings wildlife into closer contact with people, enabling deadly viruses to pass from animals to humans.

# RECIPE FOR A HEALTHY PLANET

As the global population rises, we need to make more food with less resources. This means big changes to what we eat and how we produce food, but it's well worth it. By choosing our food with care for the Earth, we can:

- Reduce climate change

- Preserve our forests and freshwater

- Stop polluting our oceans

- Prevent extinction of wild animals and sea creatures

- Regenerate the web of life that keeps us all healthy

- Feed everyone!

## A MENU FOR A HEALTHIER PLANET

### Eat less meat and dairy
This would have the single biggest impact on reducing greenhouse gases. If everyone ate a plant-based diet, we'd need 75% less farmland than we use today. That's an area the size of the US, China, Europe, and Australia combined.

Land required to feed a person for one year:

## Change how we farm
We now know how to work the land in ways that produces more food and create less damage.

### Such as:

- **Regenerative farming:** Industrial farming using chemicals and fertilizers has exhausted the land and polluted the seas. Regenerative agriculture feeds the soil by restoring its carbon and nutrients which makes it more productive.

- **Vertical farming:** Vertical farms are like high rise buildings: you can grow crops in stacked layers. They use up less land and do less damage to wildlife and natural environments.

- **Small, local farms:** Support local communities, reduce transport emissions.

- **Reduce or cut out the need for farming animals altogether**

There are already many alternative meats that don't come from animals, such as:

### Cultured meat
No, this doesn't mean meat that has been well educated, but that has been grown in a lab!

A meat eater requires 3 acres

A vegetarian (eating eggs and dairy but no meat) requires 1/2 acre

A vegan with a completely plant-based diet requires 1/6 acre

### Green eggs and ham

There's a lot more to plant-based meat than veggie burgers! Everything from plant-based steak to porkless pies is already on the menu. Companies are even working to genetically engineer plant-based substitutes for every animal product used today.

### Bugs to the rescue

Insects are a very rich protein source and are popular snacks in many countries. They can be vertically farmed, so they take up less space and prevent precious forests from being destroyed to grow animal feed or raise animals. They can even be fed food waste.

### How you can help at home and school

- Eat up what you have in the fridge

- Eat up leftovers, or turn them into delicious new dishes

- Build a compost heap and make food for the soil

**Iseult Ward** created FoodCloud, an organization that gets food that would be wasted to people who need it. Retailers use the platform to upload food that is about to go out of date so it can be collected and distributed to charities.

> *A new kind of food, a new way of farming or food sharing...*
>
> ## How would you feed a happy planet?

# POWER OF THE OCEANS
## SAVED BY THE SEA

"Here in the future, we all know there's nothing more important than healthy oceans. These days, when we're born, we usually get given a sea creature middle name to remind us of how much we owe the oceans."

If we help the oceans to thrive, we could make this future happen...

"When we finally realized how little time was left to slow climate change, we planted mangroves, seagrass meadows, and kelp forests, which stopped Earth from getting more than 2.7°F hotter while we got everything else sorted out."

"Almost all our oceans are protected. Back then, hardly any were. Some governments agreed to protect 30%, but we said, why stop there?"

"Coral reefs are the richest of all ocean ecosystems. Jellyfish robots patrol them now, so we can act fast and make sure they never get too warm."

"Blue whales are back—as well as right whales, vaquitas, manatees, hawksbill turtles, Māui dolphins, bluefin tuna, Maltese rays, Galapagos penguins, and more. We got so many back from the brink that we still sing and dance about it!"

# OCEANS UNDER THREAT

Oceans cover almost three quarters of our planet, and they can be deeper than the highest mountains. When it comes to combatting climate change, our oceans are fighting this epic battle for us like titans.

Oceans produce more than half of the world's oxygen. They also absorb a huge amount of carbon—about 50 times more carbon than the atmosphere.

Since the beginning of the industrial revolution, it's estimated that the oceans have absorbed about 40% of all $CO_2$ emissions. They absorb more than 1 million tons of manmade $CO_2$ every hour.

## 70% OF THE EARTH IS OCEAN

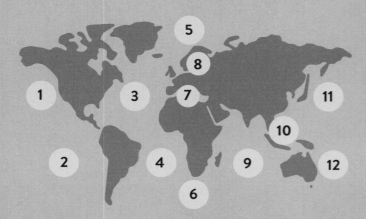

1. North Pacific
2. South Pacific
3. North Atlantic
4. South Atlantic
5. Arctic Ocean
6. Southern Ocean
7. Mediterranean Sea
8. Baltic Sea
9. Indian Ocean
10. South China Sea
11. North Pacific
12. South Pacific

## TAKING THE HEAT

The oceans have shielded us by absorbing so much excess heat on our planet, but it's taking a heavy toll. Their health is declining and they need a chance to recover...

### Meltdowns
Hotter oceans mean more risk of extreme weather events. Heat makes seawater expand and glaciers melt, so sea levels rise, endangering low-lying countries and cities.

### Food chain wipeouts
Heat can also affect currents, which carry vital food supplies through the seas. At the very bottom of the food chain, plankton is being affected. If you have no food at the bottom of the chain, almost nothing can survive.

### Acid attacks
Absorbing so much carbon makes oceans become more acidic, which is bad for shellfish and coral reefs because the acid dissolves shells and kills the corals.

### Ocean suffocation
Too much heat causes oceans to "de-oxygenate". Oxygen dissolves less well in warmer water, preventing the rich nutrients in the ocean from rising to the surface. Losing these nutrients, such as phytoplankton, means less oxygen is produced—a problem for oxygen-breathing humans!

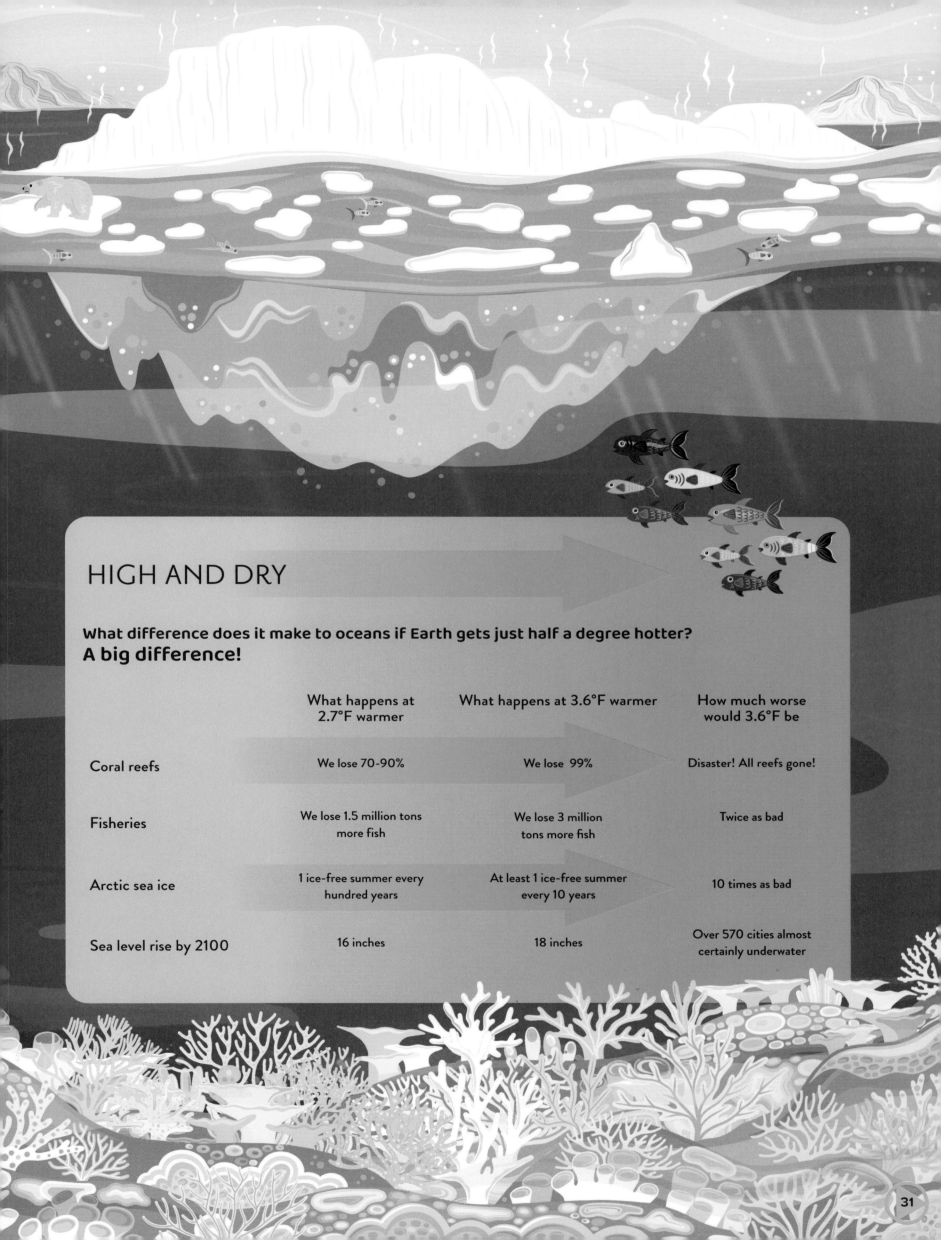

# HIGH AND DRY

**What difference does it make to oceans if Earth gets just half a degree hotter? A big difference!**

|  | What happens at 2.7°F warmer | What happens at 3.6°F warmer | How much worse would 3.6°F be |
|---|---|---|---|
| Coral reefs | We lose 70-90% | We lose 99% | Disaster! All reefs gone! |
| Fisheries | We lose 1.5 million tons more fish | We lose 3 million tons more fish | Twice as bad |
| Arctic sea ice | 1 ice-free summer every hundred years | At least 1 ice-free summer every 10 years | 10 times as bad |
| Sea level rise by 2100 | 16 inches | 18 inches | Over 570 cities almost certainly underwater |

# BLUE MAGIC

Our oceans are astonishingly beautiful, and they're home to some of the most fascinating creatures on the Earth. They have a kind of magic that helps keep our whole planet in balance.

## CARBON SINKING CHAMPIONS

Oceans are our best carbon sinks. They absorb well over a third of global $CO_2$ emissions, helping to slow down climate change. Here's how...

- Tiny plants called phytoplankton grab $CO_2$ from the air to use in photosynthesis. When they die, some sink to the deep ocean and trap the carbon there.

- Sea creatures eat the phytoplankton so, when they die and sink, carbon is stored in their fossilized bodies too.

- Many forms of sea life use carbon to make calcium carbonate, a building material for their shells and skeletons.

- Some of the $CO_2$ in the atmosphere simply dissolves in the ocean.

## BLUE CARBON

Coastal and marine plants like saltmarsh, seagrass and mangrove absorb carbon super fast—even faster than tropical rainforests. This is called "blue carbon."

- Every year, coastal wetlands capture enough carbon to offset burning 1 billion barrels of oil.

- One hectare of mangrove can offset burning 800 tons of coal (the weight of about 5 blue whales!).

- One hectare of seagrass can store twice as much as the average land forest.

- Recent studies show that oceans reduce as much carbon as is made by all the world's coal-fired power plants, every year.

# HOW TO PROTECT OUR OCEANS

**Make Marine Protected Areas**
We need to create habitats where fish can safely feed and breed, by preventing overfishing.

**Stop industrial-scale fishing**
90% of Earth's big fish are gone. Dredging and trawling scrapes up the sea bed, wrecking habitats and releasing all that stored carbon!

**Sustainable fishing**
We must respect marine habitats, and the people who depend on them. When we fish, we need to leave enough in the oceans for species to recover.

**Keep fertilizers and sewage out**
Fertilisers and sewage can cause "dead zones" where no marine life can survive.

**Ditch the plastic**
2 million tons of plastic get into the ocean every year. It kills marine life and destroys habitats.

**Keep the noise down!**
Noise from boats and military explosions can severely damage sea life.

## OCEAN HEROES

Innandya Irawan, Agung Bimo Listyanu, and Jessica Novia co-founded CarbonEthics in Indonesia. It contributes to slowing the climate crisis by restoring and conserving blue carbon ecosystems, while improving livelihoods of coastal communities.

**How you can help the oceans:**

- Talk to your parents and teachers
- Write to your politicians
- If you eat fish, make sure it comes from a sustainable source.

Agung Bimo Listyanu

Innandya Irawan

Jessica Novia

*How would you help? You can think big, and remember, many small actions make a difference too!*

# ENOUGH STUFF!
## A WASTE-FREE FUTURE

"
We didn't always throw away so much stuff, and we can get back there again...
"

"You know those days when everything breaks at once? It's one today. One company is coming to fix our waterless and another one is replacing the fridge."

"We call washing machines 'waterlesses' now as they don't use water anymore."

"Hardly anyone bothers to own appliances—we rent them now. When they get worn out, like ours, the companies replace them and re-use the parts."

# A WORLD OF WASTE

Everything goes in cycles. One lifeform is food for another. When something dies it goes into the earth to provide nutrients for something else to grow. Energy is provided by the sun without emissions to the air or our waterways. Nothing is thrown away, nothing takes more than it needs. Nature is full of transformations and regeneration. Of magic circles.

If we can learn how to work this magic, we can use it to solve some of our major problems.

## THE PROBLEM WITH STUFF

We are taught to think of ourselves as consumers, that having more stuff will make us happier or make other people think more of us. Most countries' economies are now based on people consuming as many goods and services as possible. Governments measure how successful they are by economic growth, or the amount of stuff that has been bought and sold. What they don't measure is whether this stuff has helped or harmed people and the planet.

**Stuff:**

• Makes enormous amounts of waste.

• Uses up natural resources

• Creates emissions and pollution

• If everyone lived like western consumers, we would need up to 5 planets to support us and absorb our waste. Most countries are consuming at least 3 planets' worth of resources.

Earth was formed about 4.5 billion years ago

Modern humans have only existed for about 315,000 years

More than a third of Earth's natural resources have been used by humans in just the last thirty years!

Every year we throw out over 2 billion tons of waste. This is partly because 99% of the stuff we buy is trashed within six months.

If this waste was put on trucks, they would go around the world 24 times.

## A Magic Circle

What if we thought hard and only bought things we need and created products that are not just less harmful, but actually good for the planet. How about a car that purifies the air as it drives, or a house that produces more green energy than it needs?

Right now, the way we make things is in a line, not a circle.

- We **TAKE** resources out the Earth...
- **MAKE** them into stuff...
- Then **THROW** them **AWAY** when they break or we don't want them anymore.

Take electronic waste for example:
54m tons of e-waste was generated worldwide in 2019—that's the weight of 54 million rhinoceroses!

And it included at least $10 billion worth of gold, platinum, and other precious metals.

Why not design things so the parts or materials can go back into the production system and be used to make something else, or can decompose harmlessly into the natural environment?

# BUSINESS WITH A PURPOSE

This is called the circular economy. Innovative companies are already designing products this way and are on a mission to help create a better world.

**Patagonia** is a company that says it's "in business to save our home planet." It asks customers not to buy its clothes unless necessary, and offers to help repair or find a new home for them.

**Interface** aims to be a company that regenerates the Earth. They make flooring out of recycled material using everything from windscreens to discarded fishing nets. This recycling can also help people earn an income, and save sea creatures from harm.

# HOW CAN WE WASTE LESS?

The word "economy" comes from Greek and means "managing the house."

Our planet is our house. As we understand more about how our world works, we understand we need different economic systems, or different ways of managing the house. We now know that how we make things and make money are destroying the natural world that we depend on to keep us alive and still leaves many of us in poverty. We can't have a system based on limitless growth when the planet does not have limitless resources. You don't have to be particularly good at math to figure out that doesn't add up. When the planet runs out of resources, what happens?

## DOING THE DOUGHNUT

Fortunately, brilliant economists like Kate Raworth are developing the tools that will help us to manage our house better. Kate is teaching us to do the doughnut.

- The hole in the middle is the place that people fall into when they do not have enough of the things that every person needs to live, like food, money, water, education, and healthcare.

- The doughnut itself is where we want everyone to be. It's a safe and kind place for us all to live where we look after our planet and share our wealth fairly.

- We want to get everybody out of the hole and onto the doughnut. We need to do this without using up too many resources and causing problems with the planetary boundaries we see on the ring outside the doughnut.

- The outer ring keeps the doughnut in shape. If we push these boundaries too far, we have effects like climate change, species loss, and damaged oceans. The whole planet goes out of balance.

Our challenge of the 21st century is getting better at doing the doughnut.

Here's the doughnut:

At present, we're not doing the doughnut too well. It looks like this:

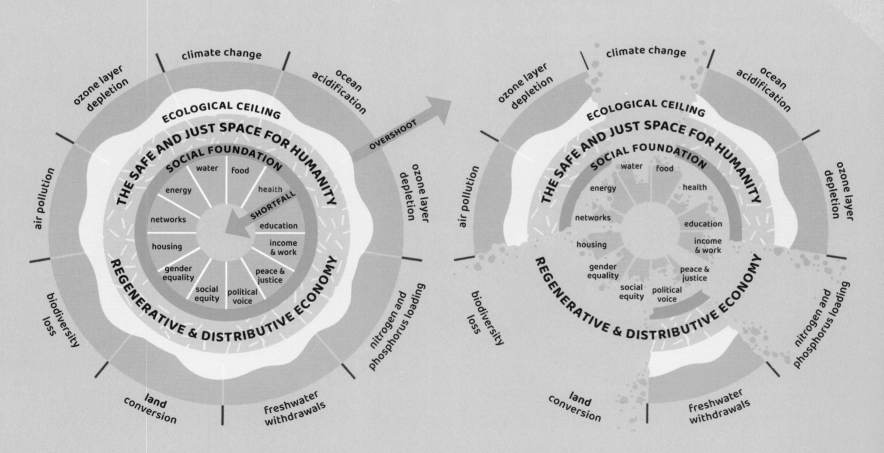

There are billions of people in the hole and we have already gone over safe limits in at least four of the planetary boundaries:

- **Climate change**
- **Biodiversity loss**
- **Land conversion**
- **Excessive fertilizer use** pollutes the air and damages oceans and freshwater (nitrogen and phosphorous loading)

## SAFE BOUNDARIES

We need to meet the needs of all people, while coming back within safe boundaries for our planet. The good news is we know how to do this and everyone can help.

**Companies can**—by transforming to circular models that use resources wisely and distribute wealth more fairly.

**Governments and banks can**—by helping these kinds of companies to grow instead of putting their money into fossil fuels and other damaging companies.

**We can**—by buying from these companies, setting them up, or working for them ourselves when we grow up, and not buying things we don't need.

**The magic is starting to work**
It's not just companies like Interface and Patagonia. Countries like Costa Rica, and cities like Amsterdam, are learning how to do the doughnut. With doughnut economics and a circular economy, we can learn how to transform and regenerate, just like nature does.

## RECYCLING HERO

When Madhav Datt was eight, he founded an environmental club at school in India called Green the Gene. It's now one of the world's largest completely youth-run environmental companies, building low-cost technology solutions for local communities facing environmental crises, across 62 countries with over 7000 young volunteers. This includes smart solutions like recycling swimming pool water and planting millions of trees.

> *How do you think we can get better at doing the doughnut? If you set up a company, what would be your purpose be?*

# AN EXCITING JOURNEY

Probably nothing has influenced the destiny of our world more than travel, for exploration and discovery, trade, war, colonization, or simply going on holiday.

Our modes of transport have set the limits and aspirations of our civilizations. From the first dugout canoes to the great sailing ships, from horses to steam trains, from carriages to cars, from trains, to airplanes, to rockets—our sense of who we are, and our imaginations, are inspired by how we can get around our planet, or beyond.

We have looked farther into unknown galaxies than humans at any other time. We know that there are limitless possibilities and that for Earth to remain a healthy part of this incredible universe, we now need to reimagine how we travel on planet Earth. And who could ask for a more exciting journey?

## Top tips for planet-friendly travel

- Take buses, trains, and other public transportation to cut pollution and congestion. These are going green fast. Look out for electric trolley cars, buses, and trains.

- Why not cycle or walk? Physical inactivity kills over 5 million people a year—that's almost as many as smoking! And 60% of car trips are for less than 2 miles.

- Get some 'E-xtra' oomph! Electric bikes give you extra power to travel longer distances, and can carry heavier loads.

- Go local. Go slow. Explore your own region for vacations, by walking, cycling, or sailing.

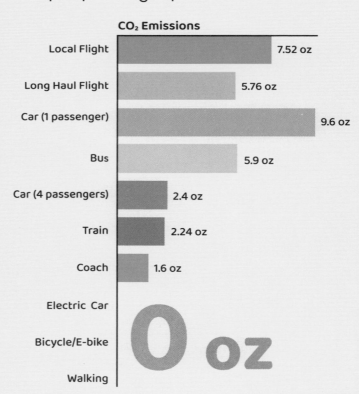

## ARE YOU A BIGFOOT OR A LIGHTFOOT?

Your carbon footprint is the amount of greenhouse gases released into the atmosphere by the things you do, for example, the transportation you use, or how you heat your house.

Almost a quarter of all $CO_2$ emissions into Earth's atmosphere come from transportation. Choosing greener ways to travel is choosing a brighter future.

**A quarter of the world's $CO_2$ emissions come from transportation.**

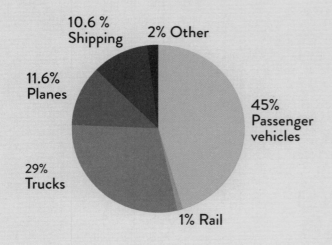

- 10.6 % Shipping
- 2% Other
- 11.6% Planes
- 45% Passenger vehicles
- 29% Trucks
- 1% Rail

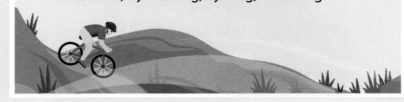

## EMISSIONS
### per passenger per mile traveled

**CO₂ Emissions**

| | |
|---|---|
| Local Flight | 7.52 oz |
| Long Haul Flight | 5.76 oz |
| Car (1 passenger) | 9.6 oz |
| Bus | 5.9 oz |
| Car (4 passengers) | 2.4 oz |
| Train | 2.24 oz |
| Coach | 1.6 oz |
| Electric Car | |
| Bicycle/E-bike | **0 oz** |
| Walking | |

## THE PLANE TRUTH

Air travel is the most polluting form of transport per passenger, per mile. These machines are starting to change all that...

### Solar Impulse
**The Solar Impulse is the first solar-powered plane to fly around the world.**

Planes taking people on holiday or on business trips generate 2.4% of all global $CO_2$ emissions from fossil fuels. That's 1012 million tons a year or, very roughly, the weight of 400 million elephants.  More people than ever are flying, so this is set to triple by 2050—that's over a billion elephants' worth of $CO_2$ in the atmosphere!

### KLM flying V
**The KLM flying V will carry 315 passengers. With improved aerodynamics, it will reduce emissions and be able to use synthetic fuel.**

Aircraft manufacturers are working on solutions to pioneer the future of planet-friendly flying. They know this is the challenge of a lifetime and are going all out to develop commercial planes that can fly on 100% biofuel or hydrogen within the next 10 years, among other brilliant innovations.

### Airbus ZeroE
**Airbus is working on the ZeroE plane, which will use a hydrogen-fueled propulsion system.**

# FUEL FOR THOUGHT

While battery-powered cars and bikes are already here, airplanes and cargo ships travel much longer distances and so need batteries that can store far more energy than possible at present. New fuels are being developed including:

### Synthetic fuel

Using hydrogen and carbon dioxide already in the atmosphere to power combustion engines so they have no carbon footprint.

### Biofuel

Made from vegetable oil, animal fats, sugarcane, waste and other sources. Jet fuel can already be partly blended with biofuel.

## GETTING SHIPS INTO SHAPE

How does chocolate get to you? Or your clothes, or your TV? As well as traveling ourselves, almost everything we eat or use has traveled, often from far away and usually by ship. Shipping is one of the world's most polluting industries, belching out tons of greenhouse gases and chemicals that cause breathing diseases. But it can get better...

The **Hydroville**, which is fast, silent and produces zero pollution, is the world's first seafaring vessel to burn hydrogen in a diesel engine.

**Green hydrogen-based fuels** are seen as a zero-emission solution for some in the shipping industry. Others are planning to replace engines with **batteries, natural gas, and biogas**, made from organic waste such as dead fish!

## GAS GUZZLERS

Do we really need 3000 lb of car to move a couple of humans and some groceries? We are seeing incredible innovations in cars to move beyond the gasoline-powered ones most of us use today. Cars can be electric, or maybe even solar powered, like the Aptera solar vehicle...

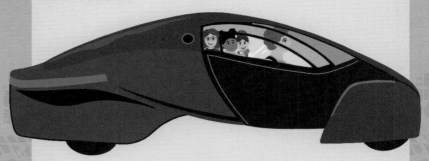

The **Aptera** is the first electric solar vehicle that requires no charging for most daily use.

### Do we really need one car each?

Around 60% of car or van journeys only have one person in the vehicle!

Cars consume a lot of energy before they ever make it to the road. Building them uses up huge amounts of resources like steel, rubber, glass, plastic, and paint. With a growing global population, will we even have room for all those cars without having to turn the whole planet into roads?

Electric vehicles (EVs) do solve some of the problems with cars, but as well as rethinking how we design and power cars, it's time to rethink owning them.

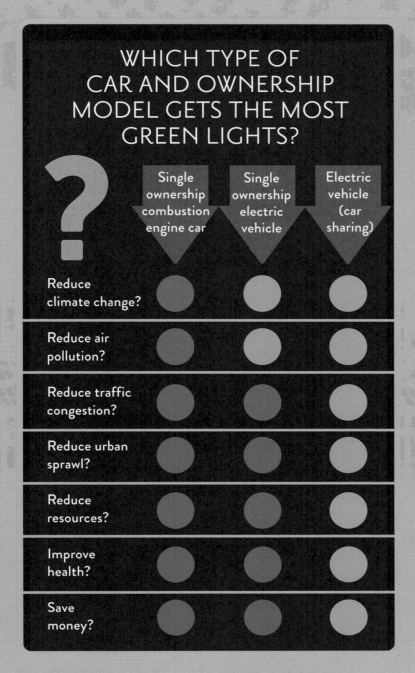

## WHICH TYPE OF CAR AND OWNERSHIP MODEL GETS THE MOST GREEN LIGHTS?

| ? | Single ownership combustion engine car | Single ownership electric vehicle | Electric vehicle (car sharing) |
|---|---|---|---|
| Reduce climate change? | ● | ● | ● |
| Reduce air pollution? | ● | ● | ● |
| Reduce traffic congestion? | ● | ● | ● |
| Reduce urban sprawl? | ● | ● | ● |
| Reduce resources? | ● | ● | ● |
| Improve health? | ● | ● | ● |
| Save money? | ● | ● | ● |

Many people are joining car clubs or car sharing programs where you can avoid all those problems and get a car on demand!

### Adventures for life

We all love going on vacation. Billions of us take vacations all over the world and this number will grow. Aside from greenhouse gas emissions, beautiful and fragile parts of the world suffer because too many people travel to them or they harm the environment when they get there. Covid 19 caused much travel to stop. This has given the tourism industry the chance to figure out how to transform vacations so they look after the planet and livelihoods of people in the destinations we visit.

## TRANSPORT HERO

**Wubetu Shimelash** co-founded Simien Eco-Trek in Ethiopia. It provides tours of the Simien mountains that create jobs for people in local communities and has enabled them to have solar lighting and to build a school.

### How about you?

What kind of machine would you design for the future? Or if you were a travel agent, what sort of vacations would you create for your customers?

# RAINFORESTS REGENERATED
## RECOVERING ECOSYSTEMS

"In our time, much of the earth's rainforest is being destroyed. Imagine if we let it grow again..."

"Wow, it's busy in here! That blue morpho is slurping, flitting, and pollinating like crazy. Its wingspan is as big as your hand!"

"That leaf beetle and those stinkhorn mushrooms are recycling, turning dead leaves into food for the soil."

"Since rainforests have been protected and properly managed, so much has regrown, but some areas still need replanting. Indigenous people are leading this work. Thanks to their knowledge we've made great progress."

"That sloth's fur is home to an entire ecosystem. No wonder he's tired!"

"Those scarlet macaws, gobbling mangoes, are helping spread seeds by dropping the stones. Seed spreading is an important part of helping the forests grow back."

"Without logging, mining, and wildlife trafficking, the jaguars are back in control, eating smaller creatures who eat plants. This means less plants get eaten and everything stays in balance."

"Our cousins the mountain gorillas in the Congo rainforests, and the orangutans in Borneo, are thriving now they've got their homes back. Their natural predators, the leopards and tigers, are back too—as they say, that's the web of life!"

# ENVIRONMENT IN DANGER

Can you imagine if somebody walked into a beautiful cathedral or temple and started to smash it down? Everyone would get very upset and the person doing it would probably have to go to jail. For indigenous communities, rainforests are sacred places, and for good reason. They are vital to life on Earth.

When we see indigenous people fighting to defend the rainforests, they are fighting for us all. At present, the law mostly allows people to destroy these essential places, but things are starting to change. The best way to regenerate the rainforests is to work with indigenous people. They have taken good care of rainforests for thousands of years, as they know their lives depend on them.

## THE WORLD'S RAINFORESTS

There are two types: temperate rainforest, mainly found in cooler, coastal areas; and tropical rainforests in warmer climates.

**Rainforests:**

- are one of Earth's richest and oldest ecosystems. Some originated more than 70 million years ago—from the time of dinosaurs!

- help stabilize the planet's climate. They absorb vast amounts of $CO_2$ and convert this into oxygen, making about 40% of the air we breathe.

- help keep the world's water cycle in balance by adding water to the atmosphere through transpiration which creates clouds. This water travels around the world.

- get about 33 feet of rain per year (about twice the height of a giraffe!). This helps create incredible biodiversity, which means many different kinds of life.

- make up about 6% of Earth's surface, but are home to over half of the world's plant and animal species.

- provide food and valuable medicines.

- help cultures to value girls, who participate in sustainable clothing and food creation using rainforest resources.

## Major Rainforests

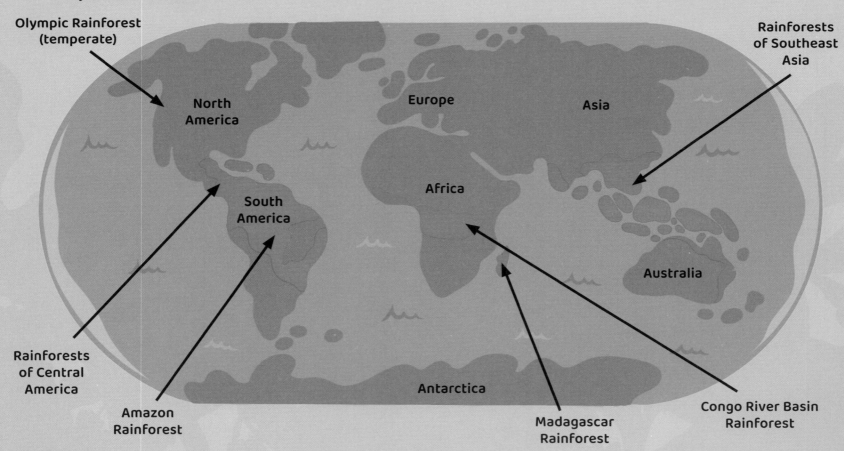

Olympic Rainforest (temperate)

Rainforests of Southeast Asia

North America

Europe

Asia

South America

Africa

Australia

Antarctica

Rainforests of Central America

Amazon Rainforest

Madagascar Rainforest

Congo River Basin Rainforest

# STOP RAINFORESTS BECOMING FAST FOOD

**Rainforests are rapidly disappearing because of human impacts such as:**

- being converted to pasture for cattle grazing—often for fast food burgers!

- growing palm oil, which is in many foods like ice cream, chocolate, pizza, and products like shampoo.

- logging for wood, used in furniture.

- being developed for housing, airports, mines, and landfills.

At the current rate, rainforests that have survived millions of years may disappear within the next century.

### Shrinking forests
About 50 million people live in tropical rainforests, including **Chief Raoni Metuktire**'s people. Chief Raoni is chief of the Kayapo people, in Amazonia, Brazil. He has been fighting to save the Amazon for more than half a century.

### What's happened to the Amazon since Chief Raoni first called for help?
An area of Amazon rainforest roughly the size of a football field is cleared every minute, according to satellite data. Since 1978, over 386,000 square miles of Amazon have been destroyed. That's one and half times the size of Texas!

**So how can we regenerate rainforests across our world?**

# DOWN...BUT NOT OUT

Tropical forests are resilient. When the forest is cleared, as long as some remnants are left that provide seeds, and enough living space for creatures who spread seeds, tropical forests can grow back with astonishing speed.

Costa Rica has regrown large areas of rainforest in a few decades after suffering some of the worst deforestation in the world. The forests are now a big part of Costa Ricans' livelihoods, including as a top spot for ecotourism.

# CONSERVATION HEROES

Who do you think does one of the most important jobs in the world...a president? A prime minister? Or could it be Chief Raoni?

Indigenous people are only 5% of the world's population, yet their traditional lands hold 80% of the planet's biodiversity. Often at the front line of defending the planet, they are doing some of the most important work on Earth.

As Covid 19 has made us aware, when forests and ecosystems are destroyed, viruses spread from animals to humans. Science now understands the role that forests play in preventing climate change, but indigenous people have long known that forests "hold up the sky."

## UNITING ACROSS THE WORLD

### Nemonte Nenquimo

In 2019, in Ecuador, Nemonte Nenquimo, a leader of the Waroni people, won a legal battle that protected half a million acres of Amazon rainforest from oil drilling and set the stage for saving another 7 million. Nemonte said, "This victory is for my ancestors. It's for our forest and future generations. And it's for the whole world."

### Chief Raoni

Chief Raoni has called for a global alliance of defenders to protect and restore the forests of Asia, Africa, and South America.

In 1993, Chief Raoni's campaigning led to the creation of the world's largest rainforests reserve in his native Brazil. He hasn't stopped since and has become a much loved symbol of resistance to the destruction of the rainforest.

### Neema Namadamu

Neema Namadamu works to protect the rainforests of the Congo Basin, the second largest on Earth after the Amazon. She helps to organize local Maman Shujaa, or "Hero Women", to protect old growth forests, reforest damaged lands and to earn a living from forests and has started tree nurseries for medicines, food, and reforestation.

# BEING PART OF BIG CHANGE

Very sadly, front line defending of the rainforest is at present difficult and dangerous work. Logging and mining companies who profit by clearing the land will sometimes go to terrible lengths to get rid of the defenders and they are often killed. In 2019, it is estimated that four environmental defenders were killed every week.

The rainforests belong to us all. By working across nations, we can save them. We need big changes to international laws to fully protect the rainforest as national governments sometimes do little to protect the defenders. The good news is that people are hard at work on this and in the meantime, there are many other things we can do. We can:

- vote for governments who will protect our planet's vital systems. Imagine voting for a president who said they'd sell our lungs? Just crazy!

- slow down deforestation, by helping people improve the way they earn a living without destroying the rainforest.

- sustainably manage forests, retaining their biodiversity and ability to regenerate.

- educate people to change how we value natural resources— learn to live with nature, not from nature. Like Costa Rica!

- protect indigenous people like Chief Raoni. We can work with them, and learn from them how to take care of the forest for future generations.

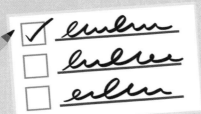

## WHAT CAN YOU DO?

- Check where things you eat and use come from.

- Choose paper and wood products certified by the Forest Stewardship Council (FSC)— like this book!—which guarantees that forests are being managed sustainably.

- Ask retailers and manufacturers to use palm oil from sustainably managed forests.

" You don't have to live in the rainforest to help defend it. Chief Raoni is getting very old, and he tells young people he meets, "I pass my fight to you." **How would you be part of the alliance of forest defenders?** "

# BUILDING THE FUTURE
## HOW OUR CITIES COULD BLOOM

"In the future, we reinvented cities to look very different—and work in harmony with nature.

"Nearly all our buildings are living now. That means they generate their own energy, collect and treat their water, and work in harmony with nature. We all have solar panels or a wind turbine or two, which collect energy to power our homes."

"Some people have a water wheel to make hydro energy. Some of us heat and cool our houses with geothermal energy from the ground."

"Quite a few people use biogas to make their electricity, which is a fancy way of saying they get it from poop. We make far more energy than we need, so we sell it back to the power companies!"

# OUR URBAN WORLD

Cities have always been at the heart of how we live. They've shaped the kind of world we live in.

That's why working out how to design cities for the future is so important, and exciting! Cities are hotspots for new ways of doing things, with tremendous power to influence and transform.

Half the world's population live in cities. This is expected to rise to almost two thirds by 2050! So if we evolve and build our cities right, we'll be a long way to getting things right for a happy planet.

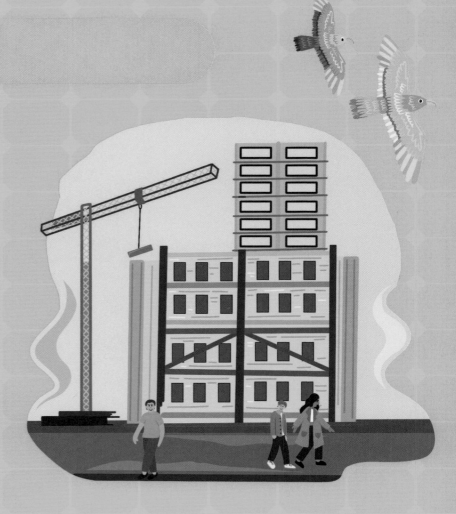

## ON THE MOVE

We need cities where everyone can thrive without using more resources than our planet has. People moving to cities is called urbanization. Let's take a look at some of the pressures rapid urbanization causes, so we can figure out the solutions.

The world's cities take up just 3% of the Earth's land, but use up 60-80% of all the energy in the world and produce 75% of global carbon emissions.

## RAPID URBANIZATION CAUSES:

- More traffic, worsening climate change and air pollution.

- Urban sprawl, with many people forced to live in poverty or slums because space for housing becomes very expensive, and wages are not always fair.

- Overconsumption—people buy more stuff when they move to cities, to feel part of (or meet the needs of) city life.

## RAPID URBANIZATION PUTS PRESSURE ON:

- Fresh water supplies

- The living environment, including animals, because green spaces are used for building

- Road and transportation systems

- Public health services

- Essential services like sewage and waste collection

# SMART CITY PROBLEM SOLVER

**Cities give us an interesting set of problems to solve. Here are the challenges...**

**Create enough room for a growing population**
We can use innovative technology to build higher, use 3D printing, and make buildings designed for shared communal use.

**Stabilize climate change and lessen its impact**
We need to make green buildings, green transportation, and green spaces, and fit existing buildings with better insulation and heating.

**Get rid of slums and poverty**
Ensure all residential areas have affordable housing, pay fair wages.

**Create healthy living environments**
Cities need a lot of green spaces: vertical farms, roof farms, gardens and allotments.

**Reduce traffic and air pollution**
Cities should be well-connected with green public transport (including car sharing), with safe spaces to walk, cycle, scoot and hoverboard.

**Make sure there is plenty of fresh water**
We need to recycle water, catch rainwater, and enable people to measure how much water they use.

**Make sure everyone can access healthcare, schools, and essential services**
Cities should have homes close to schools, hospitals, public services, and stores (which cuts emissions too!)

**Stop everyone wasting so much stuff!**
Design a "circular economy," where everything can be reused, recycled, or composted.

# BUILDING GREEN

**What are green buildings, and what can they do for us?**

This chart shows where the world's $CO_2$ comes from. Nearly 40% of the world's energy is used up by buildings, and they produce over a third of all greenhouse gases. But we're learning from nature and designing buildings that generate their own energy, create no harmful emissions, and do quite a few other brilliant things too. Turn the page to find out how...

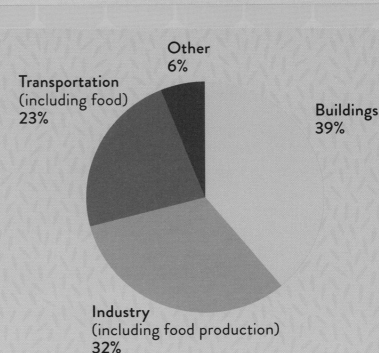

Other
6%

Transportation
(including food)
23%

Buildings
39%

Industry
(including food production)
32%

# BUILDING SMARTER CITIES

Zero carbon, or carbon neutral, buildings have solar panels and wind turbines, usually on the roof, to generate renewable power. They are built using processes and materials that create as few emissions as possible. They generate renewable energy and usually have trees or plants that can absorb carbon, so they balance out any emissions created when building them. Here are a few brilliant buildings...

### Working on Water
This floating office in Rotterdam, The Netherlands is carbon neutral and self-sufficient. That means it can supply all its own energy, water, and sewage needs. It's also "climate resilient"— it can be moored in a river, and can cope with floods and rises in water levels.

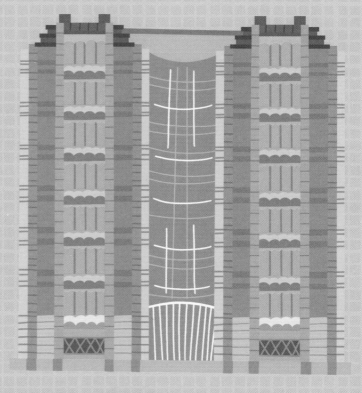

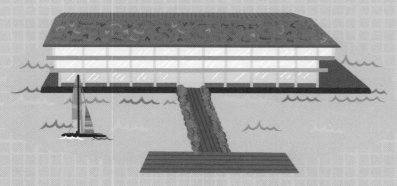

### It's alive!
The BIQ building in Hamburg, Germany is powered by algae. Tiny green algae in its outer walls eat carbon dioxide, and absorb sunlight creating energy for the building. The algae can also control light, provide shade, and even produce food!

### As cool as a termite!
Some buildings are going even further and copying nature to solve a range of problems. This is called biomimicry. Eastgate, in Harare, Zimbabwe regulates its air-conditioning and heating all year round without using any air-conditioners or heaters. Its design is inspired by the way termites cool their mounds.

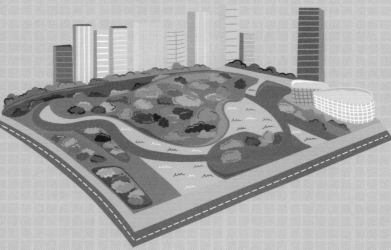

### Sponging it up!
China is developing "sponge cities" that can cope better with storms, drainage, and water shortages. They prevent flooding by replacing concrete pavements with wetlands, green rooftops, and rain gardens. This means stormwater is absorbed back into the land, and goes to work for the city. Instead of flooding, it can be used to water gardens or refill the water supply.

## STREETS AHEAD

Streets aren't just for cars, they're for people too. We spend a lot of time worrying about how to reduce emissions, congestion, and air pollution. We are redesigning cars to be more environmentally friendly. What if we redesigned our streets too? With interconnected public transportation, we could remove most cars from cities and have more space for people to walk, meet, and cycle, and for children to play.

## CITIES FOR HAPPY CITIZENS

We want our cities to be prosperous, but economic growth needs to happen without harming the planet and to be understood as a way to make sure everyone is taken care of. Perhaps the biggest challenge to creating our cities for the future is how we measure if they are blooming.

As you can see, solving problems for cities takes many different kinds of people: gardeners, architects, artists, engineers, builders, carergivers, economists, and more.

### CITY HERO

**Edgar Edmund** founded Green Venture Recycles in Tanzania when he was only 15. As a boy, he saw how floods destroyed mud houses in his city, Dar es Salaam, leaving many people homeless. Plastic littered the city too. Edgar realized he could solve both problems at once, and his company now makes bricks out of recycled plastic bags.

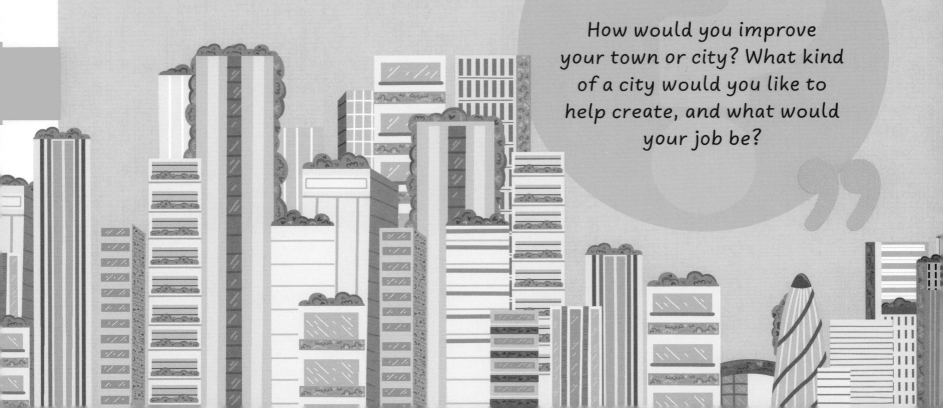

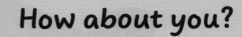

## How about you?

How would you improve your town or city? What kind of a city would you like to help create, and what would your job be?

# VOICES FOR GIRLS
## A WORLD FOR WOMEN

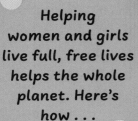

> "Helping women and girls live full, free lives helps the whole planet. Here's how . . ."

"In the future, our president has just announced that our climate is more stable, our air cleaner, our forests greener, our oceans more full of life, and most wild animals are off the endangered species list."

"The speech was streamed into our school assembly this morning, just before vertical farming. The chief scientist was speaking too. She said nearly everybody on the planet is out of poverty, all children are in school, and everybody gets healthy food, every day."

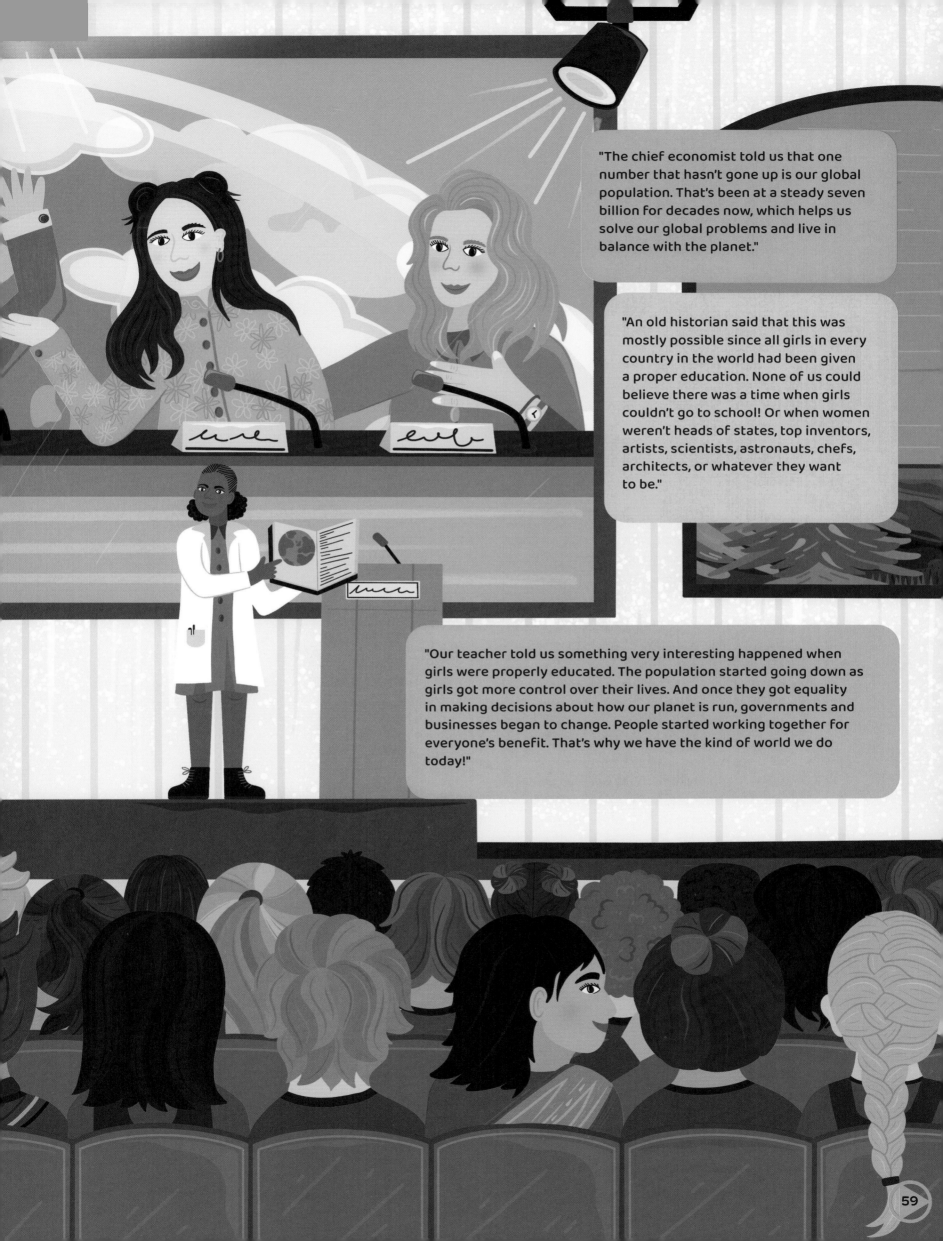

"The chief economist told us that one number that hasn't gone up is our global population. That's been at a steady seven billion for decades now, which helps us solve our global problems and live in balance with the planet."

"An old historian said that this was mostly possible since all girls in every country in the world had been given a proper education. None of us could believe there was a time when girls couldn't go to school! Or when women weren't heads of states, top inventors, artists, scientists, astronauts, chefs, architects, or whatever they want to be."

"Our teacher told us something very interesting happened when girls were properly educated. The population started going down as girls got more control over their lives. And once they got equality in making decisions about how our planet is run, governments and businesses began to change. People started working together for everyone's benefit. That's why we have the kind of world we do today!"

# WONDER WOMEN

Imagine a world without computer programming, radiotherapy, central heating, fire escapes, Monopoly, or Frankenstein!

Women created all these, and many other amazing things. But it's only recently that girls have been encouraged, or even allowed to be educated. Around the world, 132 million girls are not in school, and those who are can still face big barriers.

We can't afford to let all that brainpower and imagination go to waste. Especially when we need people who can think differently to solve our global problems.

**Keep Earth cool—send girls to school!**
Educating girls means communities are happier, healthier, and stronger, with more jobs created. And something else happens when girls go to school. Where women and girls can get an education, earn and manage their own money, and have equality and freedom, they choose to have smaller families.

## SIR DAVID ATTENBOROUGH

Sir David Attenborough is somebody who knows a lot about how our planet works. He's the patron of an organization called Population Matters which works to help girls get educated and have more choice about when and what size family they have. He says:
"All our environmental problems become easier to solve with fewer people, and harder—and ultimately impossible—to solve with ever more people."

More people mean we need to take more natural resources from Earth. We need more food, water, homes, transportation, and stuff. As we've seen in this book, these are the very things that cause more emissions, temperatures to rise, forest to disappear, animals to die, and oceans to become so overheated and polluted that they can't do their job any more.

## DOUBLE TROUBLE

The human population has doubled since 1970...and the wild vertebrate animal population has gone down by more than half. (Vertebrate means animals that have a backbone.)

10,000 years ago, almost all animals were wild. Now only 1% of wild animals are left. Without biodiversity, a rich web of life, Earth becomes fragile and survival is harder for all of us.

# OUR POPULATION MATTERS

The United Nations has calculated that if, on average, every other family had one less child than it has currently predicted (that's half a child less per family), there will be one billion fewer of us than expected by 2050—and nearly four billion fewer by the end of the century. That's a huge difference in our lifetimes!

## NO SPARE PLANET

We're using up the resources of almost two Earths. If we carry on with no change, we'll need three by 2050, or five if everyone lived like Western consumers!

The world's population is expected to reach over 11 billion people by 2100, unless we can stabilize our growth. Experts agree that, managed properly, Earth can provide a healthy diet for up to 10 billion of us, but it becomes very hard to feed everyone if there are more than that.

We all have the right to a good quality of life. So as more people around the world are able to afford more things, where are we going to find the extra planets to get all these resources from? Or the food to feed us all?

## SOLVING THINGS BY HALVES

**Expected population growth**

2100
11.2bn

2050
9.8bn

2020
7.8bn

**Half a child more**

2100
16.5bn

2050
10.8bn

2020
7.8bn

**Half a child less**

2100
7.3bn

2050
7.5bn

2020
7.8bn

**United Nations Population Projections**

# GIRLS RISE, CARBON FALLS!

For a more balanced and thriving world, we need girls to rise. Educating girls and making sure they can plan their family as they choose is one of the most powerful solutions to climate change.

## BREAKING BARRIERS
Why is it hard for some girls to get to school?

### Cost
Where school isn't free, it can be too expensive for many families.

### Long distances or poor resources
In remote areas, schools can be too far away, and some can't teach beyond a basic level.

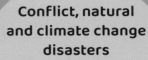

### Conflict, natural and climate change disasters
These displace many children, making education very difficult.

### Gender Bias
People in many cultures still think it isn't worth educating girls!

### Child labor
Poverty means families send girls to work, even though schools can get them out of poverty.

### Early or child marriage
Traditional beliefs and poverty means girls are forced to marry young.

Education champions around the world are working with governments, leaders, and local communities to:

- make school affordable
- help schools, and cultures, to value girls
- reduce the time and distance to get to school
- get rid of child labor, child marriage, and child poverty
- resolve conflict and provide good education for children in conflict zones and refugee camps
- stop further climate change

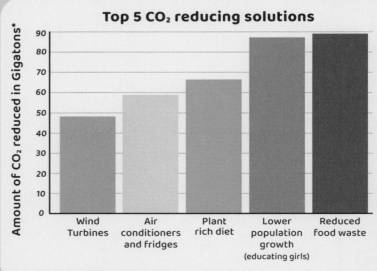

**Top 5 CO$_2$ reducing solutions**

Amount of CO$_2$ reduced in Gigatons*

| | |
|---|---|
| Wind Turbines | |
| Air conditioners and fridges | |
| Plant rich diet | |
| Lower population growth (educating girls) | |
| Reduced food waste | |

(y-axis: 0 to 90)

\* 1 gigaton = roughly twice the weight of everyone on Earth.

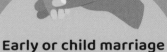

# EQUALITY HEROES

## MALALA YOUSAFZAI

**World-famous activist Malala Yousafzai says:**

"I spoke out on behalf of girls and our right to learn, in Pakistan. This made me a target. In October 2012, on my way home from school, a masked gunman boarded my school bus and asked, 'Who is Malala?' He shot me on the left side of my head. After months of surgery and treatment, I joined my family in our new home in England.

Then I knew I had a choice: I could live a quiet life or make the most of this new life I had been given. I determined to continue my fight until every girl could go to school.

With my father, who has always been my ally and inspiration, I established Malala Fund, a charity dedicated to giving every girl an opportunity to achieve a future she chooses. In recognition of our work, I received the Nobel Peace Prize in December 2014 and became the youngest-ever Nobel laureate.

I travel to many countries to meet girls fighting poverty, wars, child marriage, and gender discrimination to go to school. Malala Fund works so their stories, like mine, can be heard around the world."

## WENDO ASZED

**Wendo Aszed, the founder of the Dandelion Africa organization in Kenya, says:**

"The opportunity for education changed my life. So I founded Dandelion Africa to help other girls have the same chance. We help women and girls get an education, plan their families, and be protected from inequality and violence.

We also work with boys and men to be part of the change that will enable girls and women to be equal. We work in hard-to-reach communities and in the last three years have managed to help over 100,000 people.

People walk up to us and say 'Thank you for giving girls voices.' Girls were born with voices. They can be anything they want to be and that's why we do the work we do."

> *Educating girls plants a seed to change a community, even the world. Boys and girls are both part of this. What do you think can be done differently to make sure girls get to shine?*

# COOLING THE PLANET
## GETTING RID OF GREENHOUSE GASES

"Our emissions are helping create a dangerously hot world. So what would a future look like without them... and how would we get there?"

"It's a big clean-up! Even after we stopped most greenhouse gas emissions, there was so much of it out there that Earth was still heating. As well as not putting any more gases in, we had to get a lot out, or we could have still got more than 2.7 degrees hotter."

"Removing methane was the easiest. It's a powerful greenhouse gas, but it clears itself in about 14 years. Nitrous oxide takes about 100 years. But $CO_2$—that's carbon dioxide—and some of the others can stay in the atmosphere for hundreds, even thousands of years!"

# GHASTLY GASES

How have too many greenhouse gases gotten into our atmosphere? And can understanding this help us plan for a brighter future?

Like hot-headed outlaws, greenhouse gases can be dangerous characters when out of control. But, with a few villainous exceptions, most of them are part of Earth's natural cycles, doing an important job. They let the sun's light into Earth, and keep some of its heat from escaping. Working like a greenhouse for plants, they keep our planet at a temperature that supports life.

Human activities are causing too many of them to be on the loose. How can we round them up?

## WANTED
### METHANE—ALIAS: CH₄

**Identity:** 1 part carbon, 4 parts hydrogen

**Origin:** Cow burps, wetlands, production of natural gas, coal, and oil, decay of organic waste in landfills, and some farming.

**Troublemaking:** The second biggest greenhouse gas. It traps even more heat than CO₂ and causes about a quarter of manmade global warming.

**Troubleshooting:** Stop using fossil fuels. Eat less red meat, because less cows means less methane. Separate waste properly, and don't put biodegradable waste in landfill.

## WANTED
### CARBON DIOXIDE—ALIAS: CO₂

**Identity:** 1 part carbon, 2 parts oxygen

**Origin:** Decaying and living plants and animals, volcanoes. Burning fossil fuels.

**Troublemaking:** A major contributor to global warming.

**Troubleshooting:** Stop burning fossil fuels. Use solar, wind, and other types of energy.

## WANTED
### NITROUS OXIDE—ALIAS: N₂O

**Identity:** 2 parts nitrogen, 1 part oxygen

**Origin:** Fossil fuels and fertilizers. Also occurs naturally in Earth's nitrogen cycle: bacteria in soil and water, particularly oceans, can make it.

**Troublemaking:** Powerful greenhouse gas, third biggest contributor to global warming. Damages the ozone layer, unbalances the natural nitrogen cycle.

**Troubleshooting:** Stop burning fossil fuels. Don't use nitrogen fertilizer—shift to more planet-friendly farming.

# WANTED

## OZONE—ALIAS: O₃

**Identity:** 3 parts oxygen

**Origin:** High in the atmosphere, ozone protects Earth from the sun's ultraviolet light which can harm our skin. In the atmosphere's lowest level, it comes from cars, factories, and power plants.

**Troublemaking:** When it's lower in the atmosphere, it acts as a greenhouse gas.

**Troubleshooting:** Stop burning fossil fuels. Use transportation powered by renewable energy. Cycle and walk when possible.

# WANTED

## WATER VAPOR—ALIAS: H₂O

**Identity:** 2 parts hydrogen, 1 part oxygen

**Origin:** Water. It evaporates from oceans, rivers, lakes, and even kettles.

**Troublemaking:** As Earth gets hotter, more water evaporates, so more vapour is produced. This traps more heat and causes more warming! Warmer air can hold more vapour, leading to severe weather events.

**Troubleshooting:** Stop Earth from heating by cutting greenhouse gas emissions.

# NOT WANTED

## CHLOROFLUOROCARBONS—ALIAS: CFCs

**Identity:** 3 parts chlorine, 1 part carbon, 1 part fluorine

**Origin:** Manmade for use in things like spray cans, fridges, air conditioning, foam packing, and insulation.

**Troublemaking:** In use since the 1930s, these gases caused so much damage to Earth's ozone layer that they got banned in 1996. There are still some remaining in the atmosphere and some in use, illegally. They're powerful greenhouse gases.

**Troubleshooting:** They must go! We need to stop all CFC use and manufacture, and instead use planet-friendly alternatives such as natural refrigerants, which use gases that do not damage the ozone layer or contribute to global warming.

# NOT WANTED

## HYDROCHLOROFLUOROCARBONS —ALIAS: HCFCs

**Identity:** 3 parts chlorine, 1 part carbon, 1 part fluorine, 1 or more parts hydrogen

**Origin:** Manmade, and as dangerous as their name is long. Used to replace CFCs found in air conditioners, chillers, and fridges.

**Troublemaking:** While not as damaging as CFCs to the ozone layer, they are extremely powerful greenhouse gases. They can be 150 to 5,000 times more powerful than $CO_2$!

**Troubleshooting:** Phase out as quickly as possible. Change to natural refrigerants.

Now we know how stop them from getting out of control, let's find out where the trouble started...

# INDUSTRY: FRIEND AND FOE

The Industrial Revolution, from the 1750s to the 1850s, is the period in history that changed how things were made—and caused some of our problems...

## COAL MINING

It all started with coal. In Britain, where the Industrial Revolution began, the population was growing and people needed more fuel. Wood had been used till then, but coal produced far more energy. Coal mining was slow and dangerous though, as the mines often flooded.

**A steam engine was invented to pump water out of the mines.**
This meant coal could be mined more deeply and quickly, providing what seemed like a limitless supply of energy.

Steam-powered machines became more sophisticated and were adapted to many uses, speeding everything up. Instead of people making things by hand in small workshops, machines began to manufacture goods in factories, much more quickly and cheaply. Huge amounts of fuel were needed to drive these machines, increasing demand for coal.

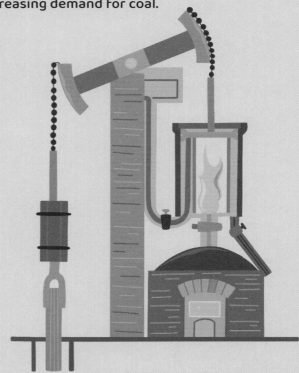

As people came from the farms and villages to work in factories, cities grew. While many worked in terrible conditions, some grew wealthier and wanted more stuff, driving even more demand for the things being produced in factories, driving more demand for coal.

In search of ever-bigger markets, the industrial barons began exporting their goods across the British empire. Other countries were quick to follow. The Industrial Revolution spread across the world, creating even more demand for coal.  It also meant that economies became based on creating mass demand for industrially-produced things...whether people really needed them or not.

Since the Industrial Revolution, greenhouse gas levels have risen steeply, driving Earth's temperature up the roller coaster we saw on page 11. By the late 1890s, scientists were aware of the greenhouse effect, and knew that burning coal made Earth hotter. By 1965, it was clear this was becoming a problem. Electric cars had existed from the 1900s, but disappeared by the 1930s as gasoline engines became more powerful and oil got cheaper. Few people considered what this might really cost...

# THINKING SEVEN GENERATIONS AHEAD

The Industrial Revolution did bring progress in many areas, though we now realize the effect it had on our climate and natural resources.

This is teaching us to think differently. Many indigenous cultures believe that you must plan seven generations ahead and investigate what impact the way we do things today will have in 150 years. So we need to make decisions thinking of our children...and our children's children!

How do you think the world would be different now if people had thought seven generations ahead during the Industrial Revolution?

## ROBOT REVOLUTION

We are rapidly discovering new technologies that are changing our world fast, just like the Industrial Revolution did. We have the chance to think hard about how these will affect us in the longer term. For example:

- What do you think about robots?
- Will they be our best friends?
- Will they form their own armies?
- What will humans do when robots can do many of the jobs we can?

How we design and programme them now, how we control the intelligence they can develop, and how we plan to make sure humans have meaningful work, will all make a difference in years to come. By learning a lesson from the Industrial Revolution and greenhouse gases, we can make better choices for our future world.

# CLIMATE HERO

Young people are asking world leaders to think now for future generations. Fridays For Future is a movement, begun in August 2018, after then 15-year-old **Greta Thunberg** and other young activists sat in front of the Swedish parliament every school day for three weeks, to protest against the lack of action on the climate crisis. Greta posted what she was doing on Instagram and Twitter and it soon went viral.

This call sparked an international awakening. Along with other groups across the world, Fridays for Future has inspired over 14 million people, in 7,500 cities and all continents to take action on the climate crisis.

> Many of us are working toward a new type of revolution, based on renewable energy and using Earth's resources much more sustainably. What are your revolutionary ideas?

# DARE TO THINK DIFFERENTLY
## OUR HAPPY FUTURE!

"Our planet is our life support system, and it could look like this—if we all take a wider view.

"It's a great view of our brighter planet from up here, isn't it? Our Healthy Happy Home (HHH) index really helped us think differently about the Earth. We use it to measure if the planet is healthy, how happy people are, and if people and animals have a decent home."

"We used to judge things by how much money each country was making, but that didn't help save people or the planet. The funny thing is, we had space-age technology even back then, but it wasn't the tech that saved us. It was how we started to think. We finally realized that our planet is the only life support system in the whole known universe!"

"We realized our best chance would be to make sure our natural systems were kept as strong as possible and allowed to regenerate."

"Now we have a global council that helps keep Earth working properly. So countries with rainforests get paid to keep them healthy. There's a law against seriously harming nature, but that seems such a stupid thing to do that no one's been taken to the international court for years."

"Because businesses that do good for people and the planet get extra money from governments (like fossil fuel companies used to, but in reverse), the ones that polluted and made things in a harmful way went bust. Who'd want to buy things from companies like that anyway?"

# LET'S GET FIXING!

As you can see from this book, we already have the solutions we need to fix our major problems and build a much brighter world. In some ways, the most difficult problem is also the easiest to solve: it's how we think.

If the next generation of human beings grows up like you, and understands how to care for this wonderful web of life that cares for us, our world will be very different in one or two generations.

## PARASITES OR REGENERATORS?

### Predatory relationships
Where one animal hunts another, like big fish eating little fish.

### Mutualistic relationships
Where lifeforms work together to help each other flourish, like butterflies and flowers.

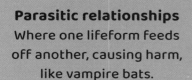

### Parasitic relationships
Where one lifeform feeds off another, causing harm, like vampire bats.

**What type of relationship do you think we should have with Earth?**

Our relationship with Earth has become **parasitic**. We are taking so much that the climate is changing, resources are running out, and species are going extinct. Parasites can play an important role in the wider ecosystem, but what happens if you are so powerful a species that you are consuming the whole ecosystem itself?

People, organizations, and countries are exploring how we can redesign our relationship with Earth to be **mutualistic**, so we work together and our future actions will help Earth stay in balance, or regenerate.

## COUNTING WHAT COUNTS

The Himalayan Kingdom of Bhutan is possibly one of the happiest countries in the world. It's certainly one of the greenest. Instead of measuring its success only by what is called GDP (Gross Domestic Product) or how much stuff is bought and sold, the King of Bhutan created a Gross National Happiness index. This counts things like sustainable development, protecting the environment and culture, and running the country well.

**Bhutan is the only country in the world to be carbon neutral, even carbon negative.**

**Here's how:**

- By law, no less than 60% of the country must be forests. So Bhutan is a carbon sink: it absorbs more $CO_2$ than it produces!

- It holds the world record for tree planting— 49, 672 in one hour!

- Logging is banned.
- Free hydroelectric power generated by Bhutan's many rivers is used instead of fossil fuels.
- All cars are planned to be electric.

Bhutan believes kindness, contentment, and living in harmony with our universe are vital to national happiness:

- Healthcare is free.
- Education for all children is free.

Like every country, Bhutan has complicated issues to deal with, but it is a compass for the world on how to reduce carbon emissions and create a harmonious and fair society.

# PARTNERING WITH NATURE

Instead of doing less harm, or even being sustainable, what if the purpose of business was to do more good? Some companies are now designing themselves so their activities are of clear benefit to people and the environment. In some cases, they make nature a business partner, using her power or intelligence to do the work.

**Changing the rules**

The kind of foundations you lay decides the type of building you can build, and the shape of a trellis decides how your plants will grow. In the same way, the kinds of rules, laws, and even language we use, shape our world. Let's think about changing the rules...

The **BeeOdiversity** organisation partners with bees to collect data about the health of the environment, to help restore the quality of soil, air, and water.

The **Ocean Cleanup** organistaion is partnering with ocean currents to clean up 90% of plastic floating in the oceans.

# JUSTICE FOR THE PLANET

Just imagine if there was a law to prevent serious harm to nature. How much easier it would be to get everyone working on cutting greenhouse gases and protecting all the oceans, rainforests, and endangered species!

Corporations and government would need to change fast, or face serious consequences. Nature, our life support system, would have a powerful friend!

When we decide something counts, we make laws to protect it. There are laws against killing or hurting someone, stealing, or damaging property. Our homes are protected, and our money, cars, and bicycles. But not our planet.

## FIGHTING ECOCIDE

Ecocide means mass damage or destruction of our ecosystems. It's not against the law. Yet. **Jojo Mehta** leads a global team of lawyers and activists at Stop Ecocide working to make ecocide an international crime. It's a big part of thinking differently and building a brighter world.

### A Global Council

Imagine you lived in a city where no one was responsible for taking away trash, cleaning the streets, or making sure everyone had clean water. You'd soon have a big mess, and probably a big fight too!

At one time, how we lived affected life in our village, town, or city. Now we're so powerful as a species that our lives affect the whole planet.

How can we keep Earth liveable and make sure there are enough resources to share now and for future generations? Just as we pay tax to a local authority to do jobs that make the community work properly, how about paying tax to a global council to take care of all life on Earth? This is called "global governance" and many remarkable people are working on the idea. Maybe you will too!

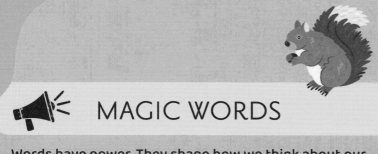

## 📢 MAGIC WORDS

Words have power. They shape how we think about our world, and how we act toward it. These words from different cultures have helped keep the environment healthy, or tried to protect people from lifestyles that destroy Earth.

### Molong

Molong means "take no more than you need" in Penan. The Penan's home is the Borneo rainforest. The Penan understand that nature must be protected for future generations. To do that, we need to learn to molong.

### See hun

See hun is another Penan magic word. It means "failure to share" and is one of the worst things you can do in Penan society, because everybody understands they need to look after the forest and each other to survive. We all depend on a healthy planet and each other, so there's no place for see hun.

### Wetiko

Wetiko is a word found in First Nations languages such as Cree or Ojibwe. Wetiko is a highly contagious virus, or spirit, that makes people think it's ok to exploit resources, animals, and other people. When indigenous Americans saw European settlers clearing forests, killing millions of animals and using other people as slaves, they believed they'd been possessed by Wetiko and feared this would spread and destroy the world. Warning their communities to beware of Wetiko was a way of teaching moderation, cooperation, and respect for all life. Let's help keep Wetiko away!

## REGENERATION HERO

**Tariq Al-Olaimy** has co-founded Public-Planet Partnerships in Bahrain to help solve our major global problems. It explores how business and governments can speed up sustainable development and regeneration, through partnerships between humans and the rest of the natural world.

> ❝ **What kind of laws or rules should we have for a brighter world?**
>
> How would you run your country or business? What new words would you invent to help us think differently? ❞

# LOOKING FORWARD

**How long will it take to fix our planet?**

Getting Earth back into balance is the most important mission of our time. If everybody worked together, how long would it take for Earth to recover?

**STOP Fast!**

## ROAD TO RECOVERY

**GO HARD!**

Here's how quickly Earth's systems can recover. We can make change if we act now.

## WE HAVE A RACE ON OUR HANDS

**Staying below 2.7°F**
We MUST stop the temperature warming by no more than 2.7°F to halt the worst effects of climate change, and keep Earth a safe place to live.

In 2018, the organization that unites the world's scientists, the Intergovernmental Panel on Climate Change, reported that we must emit no more than 420 Gigatons of $CO_2$ to stay below this limit.

We currently emit
**42 gigatons**
of $CO_2$ a year.
$420 \div 42 = 10$

That means we have **less than 10 years** to get this sorted out. We must act together, as a planet, fast! At 3.6°F warmer, the effects of climate change are much more severe. To stay below this limit, we have about 25 years.

**BY 2060**

**Ozone layer**
By 2060, the ozone layer could fully recover. It's healing well since CFCs, ozone destroying gases, were banned in 1987. It shields us from the sun's ultraviolet radiation, so would be impossible for most life to survive without it.

**WITHIN 50 YEARS**

**Biodiversity**
Sadly, 1 million species face extinction within 50 years. If we allow them to disappear, it would take 3-5 million years for Earth's biodiversity to get back to today's levels, and over 7 million to get to where they were before modern humans evolved. Evolution is a very slow process. It's vital to act while we still have time.

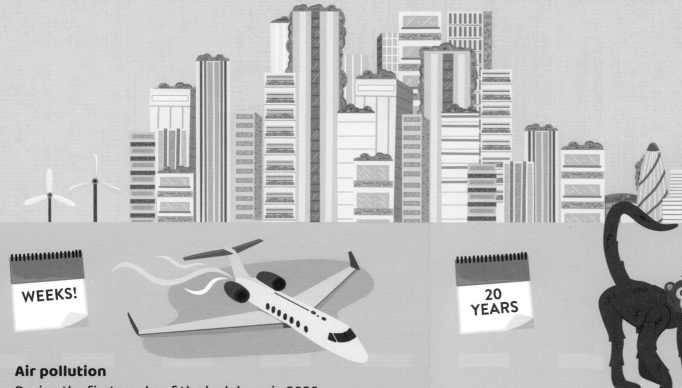

### Air pollution

**WEEKS!**

During the first weeks of the lockdown in 2020 due to Covid 19, much road transportation was halted around the world. Blue skies returned, and levels of certain gases that cause air pollution dropped by as much as 60% in some cities.

### Rainforest

**20 YEARS**

In 20 years, 80% of tree species would grow back, though it would take longer to get full abundance of plant and animal life.

### Population

**BY 2050**

By 2050 it could peak at 8.5 billion, through educating girls and access to family planning.

### Oceans

**30 YEARS**

Oceans regenerate fast, and can help stabilize the climate and provide food and livelihoods. We must protect large areas of ocean, stop polluting, stop killing sealife, and stop destroying coastal areas. It works! 50 years ago, only a few hundred of the humpback whale population that migrates from Antarctica to eastern Australia were left. Now whaling has been banned, they are 40,000 strong!

### Global warming

**DECADES**

In decades, global warming could stabilize. We can't stop it overnight, as greenhouse gases clear at very different rates and ocean currents will continue to bring heat stored in the deep ocean back to the surface. But without further emissions, this excess heat would radiate out to space and Earth's temperature would stabilize. Most $CO_2$ takes 20-200 years to dissolve into the ocean. However, some other gases can take thousands of years to clear, as they're removed by slower processes like becoming part of the rock.

> We must protect 30% of the planet by 2030 and half by 2050.
>
> By 2050, working together fast, we could have a brighter world.

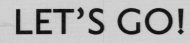

# LET'S GO!

How can we make this bright future happen?

What we choose to do over the next 10 years writes the next chapter for life on Earth. As we've seen in this book, that can be a happy one.

These are, perhaps, the most exciting times to be alive. We have great power for transformation. In this book, we've seen wonderful people on the move. Many of them started working on solutions when they were at school - maybe you can too!

Look at how much change we can make with simple actions in our daily lives! If we all get into the habit of doing these, we'll be on course for a brighter world.

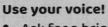

**Use your voice!**
- Ask for a brighter world.

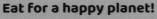

**Eat for a happy planet!**
- Check where your food, including fish, comes from.
- Eat less meat and dairy.
- Don't waste food.
- Try growing your own.
- Eat locally grown food.

**Be a carbon lightfoot!**
- Travel light, by foot, bike and public transportation.
- Save energy.
- Use renewable energy where you can.

**Wallop waste!**
- Recycle, reuse, and compost your leftovers.
- Save water.

**Say enough to stuff!**
- Don't buy things you don't need.
- Cut out single use plastic.

**Be informed!**
- Check where and how things you buy and use are made.

**Include Girls!**
- Get the world running on full brain power.

**Go wild!**
- Enjoy nature.
- Help create wild spaces, especially for pollinators.
- Volunteer for conservation and clean-ups.

**Believe you can make a difference!**
- Use how you live, your ideas and innovations to be part of the solutions.

**Care, share, dare!**
- Care for Earth, collaborate, and dare to think differently about the future you can create.

## ACTIONS MAKE CHANGE!

- **PROTECT RAINFORESTS AND FRESHWATER**
- **PROTECT OCEANS**
- **STOP EXTINCTIONS**
- **PROTECT BIODIVERSITY**
- **REDUCE CLIMATE CHANGE & AIR POLLUTION**
- **MAKE A BRIGHTER WORLD**

## KEY TO SYMBOLS

 1. Reduces emissions

 2. Less heat absorbed

 3. Prevents overfishing

 4. Prevents harm from fertilizers

 5. Stops deforestation

 6. Prevents habitat loss

 7. More food for everyone

 8. Fairer work and wages

 9. More jobs in a greener economy

 10. More freshwater for everyone

 11. Prevents plastic from killing sealife

 12. Less shipping, less pollution and noise

 13. Better sharing of Earth's resources

 14. Lower population

 15. Protects food chain

 16. Keeps you healthy

 17. Makes you happy

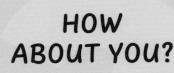

## HOW ABOUT YOU?

Think of all those brilliant ideas you've come up with while reading this book. The bright future is up to you now...

79

# INDEX

## Acknowledgments
The writing, research and the inclusion of such brilliant activists in this book
has been made possible by the help of so many wonderful people. With special thanks to:

Dr Steve Bird, Chloé Bird, Clare Brook, Joff Brown, the Colmet-Daâge family, Eliza Forde,
Marianne Gunn O'Connor, Niahm Gunn, Jane Harris, Margaret Hope, Sophie Locke, Robin Maynard, Dan Maunder,
Christine McDougall, Jojo Metha, Neema Namadamu, Amber Nuttall, Sir Jonathon Porritt, Kate Raworth,
Princess Esméralda de Réthy of Belgium, Soledad Sede, Jessica Sweidan, Alison Taylor, Antoinette Vermillye

### And to:
Amazon Frontlines, Blue Marine Foundation, Cambridge University Cambridge Zero,
Dandelion Africa Organisation, Doughnut Lab, Earth X TV, Fridays for Futures, Hero Women Rising,
Instituto Raoni, Malala Foundation, One Young World, Population Matters, Public Planet Partnerships,
Stop Ecocide, Synchronicity Earth, Women's Earth and Climate Action Network (WECAN) International

And Bethany Lord for the beautiful illustrations.
—CF

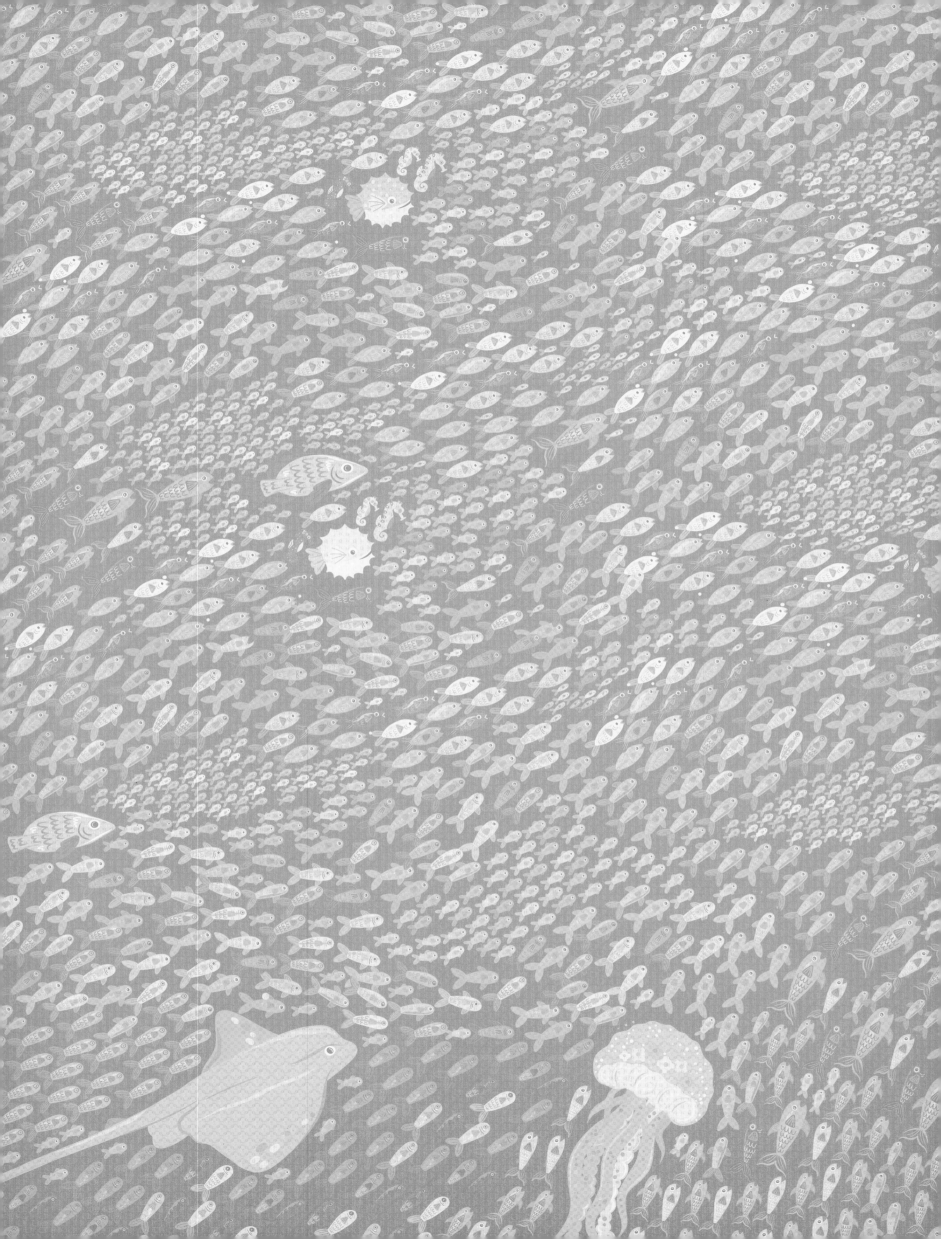